DALTON'S GOLD

PETER D MATTHEWS

Swindled out of the find of the century
by the very forces sent to protect
and uphold the law...

What's a man to do?

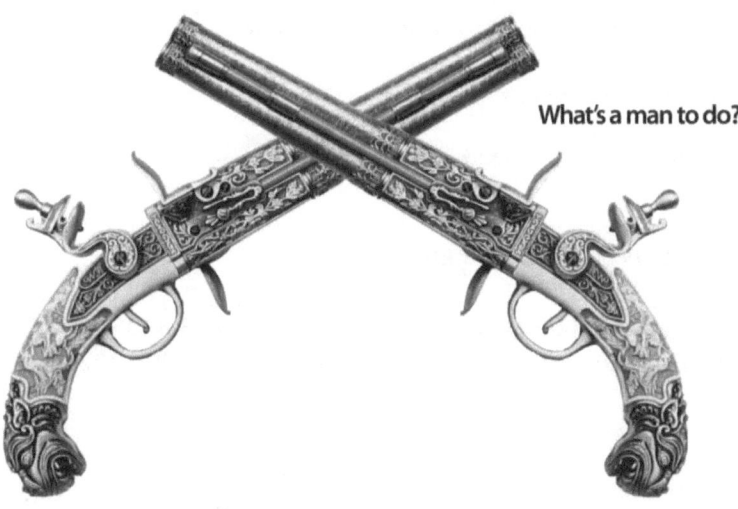

Dalton's Gold

ISBN 978-0-9873652-0-0
Copyright © 2012 Dr Peter D Matthews.
First printing 2013 (Print copy)

All rights reserved. No part of this book may be reproduced, or transmitted in any form or means, electronically or mechanically for any other means, and must be kept in its original form. This book may not be photocopied or uploading to any internet site, without the express permission in writing from the Author and Publisher.

This book is based upon a true story. Original book cover design by Deidre Stein, tweaked by Jonathan Matthews.

Bassano Publishing
P O Box 454,
Stanthorpe, Queensland 4380 Australia

Previous books by Dr Peter Matthews:

⚘ Living in the Year of Jubilee ISBN 978-0-646-34950-3
⚘ The Reformation of Australia? ISBN 978-0-646-53227-1

Look out for Peter's next books at
www.petermatthews.com.au

DEDICATION

This book is dedicated to my grandfather, Francis William Dalton who, just before he passed away in 1995, told me this very story. He knew that the seed he planted all those years ago would stay with me, grow and drive me to research, confirm, pull together, and finally mature into this amazing story.

It is also dedicated to John Thomas Dalton and his descendants, who were swindled out of their find of the century by the very forces who were sent to uphold the law.

Specifically, I dedicate this book to John Thomas Dalton's oldest living descendant, William Leonard Dalton (his grandson), aged 91, who now lives on the outskirts of Cairns with his wife Gwen, enjoying the simple life.

ACKNOWLEDGEMENTS

I must thank Peter Dalton (son of William) and his wife Denise, for their incredible assistance and support. They provided the missing links that I had been researching for three years.

Finally I must acknowledge Deidre Stein (sister of Denise Dalton) who provided the original design concept for the front cover of this book.

Thank you all so much for helping me tell this incredible tale that will rewrite the history books.

Dalton's Gold
By Peter D Matthews

TABLE OF CONTENTS

		Page
Chapter 1	The Southern Cross Calls	7
Chapter 2	In Search of Gold	19
Chapter 3	Dalton's Flat	35
Chapter 4	Secret Gold	51
Chapter 5	Quell the Digger's Indignation	69
Chapter 6	Tension Rise on Eureka	81
Chapter 7	The Southern Cross Shines	105
Chapter 8	Rebellion or Premeditated Bloodbath?	135
Chapter 9	Run For Your Life	153
Chapter 10	Revenge - A Two Edges Sword	179
Chapter 11	State Trials	201
Chapter 12	Reformation of a Nation	243
Chapter 13	Foreign Rebels or Pioneers	259
Chapter 14	Dalton's Lament	273
History Captured		279
References		280

Dalton's Gold
By Peter D Matthews

DALTON'S GOLD

by Dr Peter Matthews

    John Thomas Dalton was woken suddenly with the tumultuous sea crashing over the bow, just as the ship's surgeon dragged another lifeless body passed his bed, bumping his elbow on the way past. Twenty-five dead so far on their epic voyage to Australia, and all John could hear below deck was the sobbing and bawling from relatives of the recently deceased, preventing him from sleeping.

    Night after night he tossed and turned, wondering if he had made a mistake by boarding the ship. He had heard of the new land of Australia, and how they had found gold. A land filled with such promise and wealth, drew men from all over the world.

    John was inspired by these tales, and decided to lay down his tools as a lowly paid boot maker. Instead he would brave the high seas in search of gold; a new land; a new life; and perhaps even love.

Dalton's Gold
By Peter D Matthews

He could not afford a passage from his homeland in Canada, so instead lined up as a seaman. He boarded a ship to Liverpool, then sailed on to Port Philip Bay.

John was now twenty-two. He was a restless young man in pursuit of a dream, and the thrill of adventure. Love had not come his way in his country village of Arichat, Canada. All of his friends were married and settling down, so John headed his own way.

He was tall and lanky, but strong and fit with the body of an athlete. His physique, together with being well spoken and fluent in three languages, made it easy for him to secure free passage as a seaman.

A handsome young lad of spritely attire adorned his shapely body with a crisp white linen shirt; cream trousers; fancy cream waistcoat; all topped off with his black string tie. His hair was dark and always neatly combed. His countenance was bright, from his smooth rounded face, clean shaven except for his famous flat bottomed goatee. It almost seems like Coronel Sanders had modelled his advertising on John.

John was renowned for his shoes - his dark black, highly polished handmade dress boots set him apart from the rest. Many a gentleman asked John where he came across such an exquisite pair. He was as proud as punch to be able to say, 'I made them myself. I am a boot maker.'

Upon hearing that, he was instantly commissioned to make not just one, but a number of pairs of boots, for many astute gentlemen.

Dalton's Gold
By Peter D Matthews

'Give me a hand, laddy' said the surgeon as he struggled to drag the lifeless body past John's bed. He was a rather tactless overweight fellow with a loud Irish accent, and a good portion of English pomposity thrown in.

John reluctantly arose and helped the surgeon drag the lifeless body back near the surgeon's quarters.

A light shone brilliantly below deck of the darkened ship. A silhouette of a single still figure shone towards him from the dimly lit room beyond. It was such a sight that John could not turn away. John stood silent, captivated by the beauty of a young lady.

The surgeon wondering why John had stopped so abruptly, noticing his gaze. He snarled at John, 'Snap out of it boy. Get your eyes off my niece.'

Margaret just smiled at John, noting his affectionate gaze, returning her interest in him. Her smile was enough to light up the most dreary and ordinary day. John was left mesmerized as her bright blue eyes met his, melting his heart, and he could not turn away.

John was not hunting for, nor interested in a wife, but just at that second that his eyes met hers, he knew in his heart that she was the one - his ultimate soul mate. Yet they had not even spoken.

Waking him from his trance, she softly offered, 'Hello, my name is Margaret' with a thick Irish accent.

John had no thoughts about marriage; kids; or settling down. He was on an adventure, enjoying the bachelor life, travelling the high seas in search of fun and fortune. Falling in love was the last thing he had in mind, but that all changed in a brief moment in time.

In fear of blowing it by what he might say, all John could muster was a simple 'hello,' putting on a thick Irish accent to disguise his Canadian accent.

The Irish on board had shown John their detest of Americans and Canadians alike. After all John's parents were Irish, having settled in Canada, so he was of Irish blood. John felt it better to pretend to be Irish and woo her heart, than be rejected forever, purely because of where he was born.

Noticing the connection, Dr Carr turned to John, bearing his orders, 'Well lad - off you go then'.

John went back to his uncomfortable bed, somehow contented to have gazed deep into those beautiful blue eyes. With that thought in mind, he soon fell back off to sleep, and slept like a baby until he was due back on deck.

It was by now the 2nd October 1852. As they entered Port Philip Bay headed for the port of Geelong, John's dream came to an abrupt stop. The ship had run aground on a sand bank.

The sudden jolt sent the ship into disarray, people and cargo flung forward entangled in a haphazard mess, with passengers groaning under the weight of baggage, let alone the emotional strain. With the commotion below, the crew scampered to see what had happened. The captain realizing he had run the ship aground, trying to regain some composure, he directed the crew to lighten the load.

Dalton's Gold
By Peter D Matthews

The already intoxicated crew, singing joyful shanties, began throwing the passengers belongings over the side of the ship. The captain meanwhile sat back at the wheel and drank his sorrows into stupor.

This erupted into a fight on board between passengers and crew. The few belongings that these Irish and Scottish migrants held dear, was being discarded and tossed into the sea. They had been plunged into a world so far from what they dreamt of, when they first embarked the ship.

The fanfare and excitement at Liverpool had faded into the depths below. Realizing their imminent fate, the passengers united with the crew, throwing overboard anything they could in a desperate effort to survive.

Pure desperation drove the crew and passengers, lugging tons of cargo up onto deck and overboard, leaving not a barrel of flour, nor livestock, leaving them nothing to eat - even the biscuits were now mouldy. The port was within distant sight, but yet too far to swim.

The past three months aboard living in squaller had left them weak, frail and now hungry, with no food. They sat anxiously waiting for the tide to rise, reflecting upon the twenty-five dead, concerned now of what their own fate might hold. They hoped for a miracle, and not a watery grave.

After a tedious thirty-seven hours, the anguish turned into jubilation, as the mighty ship floated off its capture - the sand bank. The ship struggled on, eventually arriving at Point Henry in Geelong on 4th

October 1852. By the time the ship reached port, there were twenty-seven dead, plus one poor soul lost overboard.

The passengers restlessly waited for clearance to disembark the vessel. Aboard came a stern but sprightly fellow, the district surgeon W.H. Baylie. He marched up and down the decks, inspecting the jumbled hold, the recently deceased, and eventually the living. He seemed to be checking for disease. His unsympathetic words to the captain and crew were, 'This is the dirtiest ship I have ever seen abroad. The migrants are swarming with lice.'

Mr Baylie quarantined the ship for one more gruelling week. Nobody could leave the ship. With morale at an all time low and tempers flaring into rage, the ship turned into a prison. The ship was guarded day and night by 'red-toads', as the English military were called, with orders to kill anyone found fleeing. 'What a wonderful welcome to the new Victorian Colony' John thought.

Mr Baylie also recommended that Dr Carr, 'never again be given charge of a migrant vessel'.

The entire ship had to be scrubbed from top to bottom, and everything cleaned before anybody could disembark. All pitched in and eventually they were allowed to come ashore.

After the passengers and the remainder of the cargo had been removed, the ship's captain gathered the crew, including the Carr's, addressing them with a proposition. He offered to pay the crew right there and then, and then take them back up at their usual rate upon his departure; or they could go with him to the diggings at Ballarat and share in the spoil.

The captain however made agreement with the crew that the expenses for the ship be paid first, and one third of any gold found should go to the ship, and the rest distributed with those that decided to come with him.

John sat back cautiously waiting to see if Dr Carr decided to take up the offer of the captain. John was torn between his love of the sea and this new found love, Margaret. As soon as Dr Carr signalled the captain, John stood up. With his mock Irish accent in a big voice, he shouted, 'I'm in'.

The crew consisted of thirty regular hands, plus ten extras such as John. They left the ship and headed to Ballarat, over eighty kilometres of rugged terrain by horse and cart. Back in 1852, the roads were nonexistent and the only method of transport was by horse which took 3 days, or 3 weeks on foot.

Arrival at Ballarat

The climate was hard to bear, as John was accustomed to a white Christmas of minus six degrees Celsius. Instead John was welcomed to Victoria with a sweltering thirty-five degrees. His heart drew faint, wondering if he had made the right decision. He pondered his fate once again: would he find gold, or would he die of heat stroke in this scorched sunburnt land.

Dalton's Gold
By Peter D Matthews

As they approached the top of the last hill before descending into Ballarat, the town was starting to appear through the thick Australian scrub before them. There in front of them, was a clearing. The view below was an astounding sight. The green expanse of rolling hills flowed down into a magnificent green tinged lake. What a sight to a hot and sweaty traveller.

Almost overtaken by the heat, the lake was the most unforgettable, but welcome sight. The lake was surrounded with thousands of tents, bark huts, horses, wagons and bullocks. People everywhere were busy digging, moving moulds of dirt, and panning for gold. Ballarat was a striking settlement, inundated with people from all walks of life, from many parts of the globe - all to call Australia home, in search of their fortune.

Dr Carr and his wife, along with Margaret, headed straight for the hospital, where they found immediate work and accommodation. Being a ship's surgeon he was always welcomed with open arms, which allowed him free access to mine for gold without a licence.

Women, medical practitioners, and religious leaders were exempt from being required to hold a miners licence. Every other person was required to pay one pound and ten shilling sterling which allowed each person one month to search, dig and remove gold.

John and his ship mates pitched their tent, setting camp on Canadian Flat. They had just enough

Dalton's Gold
By Peter D Matthews

money to buy provisions, picks, shovels, panning equipment, and sufficient left for their gold licences.

John picked up and brought with him a newspaper that someone had left at the Liverpool dock. It was advertising the Ballarat goldfields. The advert told of gold finds – 'John Hart on 16 August 1851 of a 67 ounce nugget at Golden Point, followed by William Howe on 8 November 1851 with an 84 ounce gold nugget, also at Golden Point'.

With their gold licences, they headed off to Golden point, apart from the captain. In true captain form, he sat back and drank under the guise of supervising the crew.

They arrived on Golden Point to find scores of holes abandoned. Many diggers had already moved on, thinking Golden Point had been depleted. John jumped into a hole about five feet deep, while the others stood around watching what everyone else was doing. Along came a neighbouring digger, realising they were new at the game, and offered his assistance.

He was a short but strong stout man, with a full beard, and a rich Scottish accent. His name was James Scobie. He and his brother George had only just arrived in Australia from Perthshire, Scotland. They had just found their feet or should I say their first decent gold nugget.

James asked John to jump out for a moment so that he could show him how it was done. James jumped into the three feet diameter hole, which was about five feet deep, just to the top of his head. He fiercely swung his pick down into the hole, and 'clink' was the sound on his first hit. He reached down and came up with a small gold nugget just over an ounce (about thirty-five grams).

    John thanked him, and jumped into the hole himself. John however was over six feet tall, with a full head and shoulders out of the hole. With an almighty blow, he struck the bottom of the shaft, and there was nothing but a dull thud. He drove the pick again and again aggressively into the ground, to find nothing more than a handful of gold dust.

    Tired already from his pounding, he did not give up, but swung it again, and again, and then all of sudden, there was a 'clink'. John could see a yellowy gold flicker in the bottom of the hole. He carefully unearthed his find. Within an hour in the hole, he had found a seven ounce gold nugget.

    John jumped and danced in excitement. His eyes opened wide, glimmering like freshly polished diamonds. He had fallen head over heels in love. In love with what? Love of gold - he looked upon the gold and was somehow besotted with gold fever.

    However, the captain claimed the first find, retaining the seven ounce nugget for the ship.

    John was rather offended, as it was he that had found the nugget, while the others watched, and the captain sat back and drank. He was already owed eighty-one pound and ten shillings from the captain in wages. He demanded that the captain share the proceeds of the find with the crew or at least pay the wages outstanding.

Dalton's Gold
By Peter D Matthews

The ship's captain did neither, pushing the crew to work six day a week, working tirelessly in the gruelling mine. John had no time for play, no time for Margaret, no time for anything but strenuous, relentless digging, while the captain sat and drank the whole time.

Many of the crew found gold that week but refused to share it with the captain. The captain rose up to strike one of the crew for not surrendering the gold as he was fast losing control. Half of the crew arose against the captain to defend their mate. The captain had no choice but to back down. He departed Ballarat with only fifteen of the crew willing to go with him. He took the seven ounce gold nugget found by John, along with the crew's wages, declaring that they had refused to go with him, therefore had abandoned ship, so no wages were due.

The rest of the crew decided to split up all over the goldfields in search of gold. Each of them promised the other to let each of them know if they made any considerable find.

With what little John had to his name, he decided to stay, believing he would find his fortune.

2
IN SEARCH OF GOLD

John firmly believed he would find the 'pot of gold at the end of the rainbow'. He was so sure of himself, believing the elusive gold nugget laid in wait, hidden just for him to dig up. It was just a matter of time before he would find it.

'It might be the next stroke of the pick' he used to say to keep his spirits buoyant. It drove him to work long days, digging shafts; carting gravel; carting water; and panning in search of gold.

His mates James & George Scobie moved down to Canadian Flat and found gold at ten feet, so John following them. He built a 'slab' hut on Canadian Flat with a mud chimney on the end in preparation for winter. The diggers used rough cut slabs of timber for rough shelters, as well as shoring up the mine shafts to prevent collapses.

John worked tirelessly, starting on the right-hand side of Golden Point, climbing Canadian Gully. He stayed close to his new found mates, the Scobie brothers.

Dalton's Gold
By Peter D Matthews

Next to his claim was a refined Italian gentleman. His name was Raffaello Carboni. He was an educated man - a well spoken poet. Carboni was a declared Italian nationalist and in it for the money. He was not even considering settling in the colony of Victoria. He was merely there for the gold.

Most of the diggers John came across were either naturally born Australian, or those from abroad to call Australia home in search of a better life. Carboni was very different from most of the diggers. He talked about the renaissance, art, poetry and the finer things of life in Italy. Yet, he worked amongst the diggers of Ballarat in search of gold.

On Sundays, he wore a pair of dark black fly-front trousers with a white fine linen shirt, garnished with a black cravat around the neck, knotted in front, then tucked down into his jet black double breasted waistcoat. All this was finished with a black pardessus or formal cape, with a yoke across the shoulder line. His hat was a magnificent black broad-brimmed hat, trimmed in red, like one would wear to a formal doctoral graduation.

Even working in the pit, he wore a pair of trousers, white singlet, graced with a pair of old tattered, but handcrafted, dress boots.

He was clearly Italian, with an olive complexion, dark hair with a reddish tinge, and a red beard, neatly trimmed short. He had a hooked nose, sunken tiny hazel eyes, overshadowed by a broad protruding forehead with shaggy eyebrows.

Dalton's Gold
By Peter D Matthews

He was rather short, measuring only up to John's shoulder but made up for it with his mouth. He was known for his sharp articulate tongue that could dress down a man in seconds without having to raise a fist.

His only lack was a pair of new hand-crafted black dress boots. Carboni demanded to know where John bought his boots. Proud as punch John piped up, 'I made them myself' while chuckling to himself.

John was only interested in digging for gold, but Carboni would not take 'no' for an answer. Carboni made an agreement with John to work together in a deeper shaft, with Carboni buying the equipment, and taking half share of the spoils, less the two labourers, if John would make him a pair of boots. Carboni desired for John to secure the finest supple black Italian leather from the port of Geelong. John shook hands with Carboni agreeing to make him the finest Italian leather boots he had ever made.

Come nightfall John along with many of the diggers would come together around the fire for a drink and a meal, enjoying the company of their mates and a good yarn. He became good friends with Carboni and the Scobies, but Carboni didn't trust the Scobies at all. He made this known in no uncertain terms.

Carboni had seen them fraternizing with the local police and believed they were spies for the government. Whereas John Dalton was everybody's mate, and would do no man any wrong.

Carboni enjoyed reminiscing around the fire, eloquently speaking of faraway lands, reciting poetry and debating the arts. John and the rest of his mates sat enthralled in another of one of Carboni's stories. Carboni was overjoyed to be back at Ballarat. This group of miners where far more learned, decent and respectable diggers, than those Carboni had encountered at Bendigo.

Bendigo was hard work by day, and little sleep by night, trying to block out the music of drunken quarrels and fist fights, which was almost impossible to do. Carboni was overjoyed to return to his peaceful diggers of Ballarat, sitting around the campfires together.

Although John had many friends he could not shake his overwhelming thoughts of Margaret Carr, and the emptiness in his heart without her.

One afternoon almost on dusk, John decided to clean himself up and go to visit her. Wearing his best attire, he turned up at the hospital. It was a risk, but he just had to at least get a glimpse of Margaret. If only their eyes could meet once again? Then he would know for sure if she was the one.

John peered through the hospital window and a familiar voice called out to him. It was Dr Carr, and in his normal gruff tone, 'well, come on in lad'.

'This was my opportunity' John thought. Dare he walk away and say nothing. He decided to go into the doctor's quarters. Dr Carr invited him in to sit at an old wooden table, where Dr Carr offered him a drink.

John could clearly see that Dr Carr was already under the weather, so thought, 'Why not'.

Dalton's Gold
By Peter D Matthews

Dr Carr yelled 'Margaret, bring me another bottle of whiskey. There is a fine gentleman here to see you.'

Margaret came out rather grubby in plain clothes from doing the dishes. She placed the bottle down on the table in front of her uncle. As Margaret stood there still and silent, her eyes clearly all over John, she suddenly became self-conscious of her own attire after admiring her suitor in his Sunday best.

John did not wait for her to turn away, but looked deep into her radiant blue eyes. The moment their eyes met, Margaret's face blushed, and her eyes glimmered. John knew at that very instant that the glimmer he saw back on the ship was real, and Margaret was to be his wife.

He had hardly said a word together with Margaret. John drank his first whiskey and managed enough courage to speak with a gust of that thick Irish accent. He hastened, 'With your permission Sir, I would like to marry your niece'.

Dr Carr said, 'I promised her father, William Carr, that I would not let her marry a poverty stricken seaman or miner, of which you are both. Have you any gold boy? Can you buy land? How will you support her?'

John, in a lowly voice, sculling down his second glass of whiskey for inspiration, replied, 'No, sir, I have no gold or money to speak of, but I have love. I have loved Margaret from the first time I set my eyes upon her, and I solemnly promise to love her and protect her until the day I die.'

Dalton's Gold
By Peter D Matthews

Margaret sat quiet, just looking longingly at John, admiring his love and passion, wanting her uncle to say the words, 'Surely, lad'. But he did no such thing.

Dr Carr sat back in his chair scouring, 'When you find this gold nugget you speak so much about, then come and talk to me. You spend so much of your time looking for gold, instead of working a descent profession. Once you have started your own business to take care of my niece, then and only then young lad, can you have her hand in marriage.'

He looked longingly into the eyes of his love. John although disappointed, realising the prospect of a 'Yes', he excitedly hastened, 'I will be back for you Margaret. I will find my elusive nugget and take you as my wife'.

Margaret melting agreed, 'I will wait for you, as long as it takes'.

John, not wanting to outstay his welcome, he bid Dr Carr farewell, taking him upon his word. He strode back to his camp dreaming of how he would find that nugget and return to claim his bride.

Dr Carr's attitude towards John had somehow changed from that time onwards. He seemed to believe John's enthusiasm and passion for Margaret, thinking this motivation and determination to find gold, might actually occur.

By this time there were thousands of immigrants swarming into the camp. All came seeking a better life, and in search of the same elusive gold nugget.

Dalton's Gold
By Peter D Matthews

John had resolved in himself, come Sunday he was going to talk to the priest of St Alipius Catholic Church. He would declare his intentions in the hope that the priest would keep a eye on Margaret, and of course give a favourable mention in the ear of Dr Carr.

The entire digging stopped each Sunday as all were God fearing men. Be they Catholic or Protestant; from Ireland, England, America, Canada, Europe; it did not matter - they all observed the Sabbath.

As they all assembled, polished up in their finest apparel, after all church was the only opportunity for them to dress in their finery. The women dressed as if they were attending a ball. Most wore fine gowns of silk, with short sleeves, lace flounce collars, and long tiny pleated skirts that gathered to a pointed waist. Many wore their hair bunned or knotted, with a few long curls dangling down towards the front. Others had braids tucked into the bun. Married women particularly wore frilly linen caps with lace, and ribbons to show they were hitched. After all, with 12,000 men and 4,000 women on the goldfields, it was rather precarious for a woman to walk the streets alone.

The men were all well groomed, with the majority wearing broad-brimmed hats to allow their curly sideburns and moustaches to protrude, in an effort to be distinctly perceived as a distinguished gentleman. Some were clean shaven but the majority grew long beards, as was the fashion. Clothing had a significant part to play which set the Ballarat settlement apart from the rest. Ballarat was seen as a more civilized upper class community with impeccable morals as law abiding citizens.

But yet the English born Australian Government called them 'vagabonds', to which they all took serious offence. This was because the majority of miners were free migrant settlers or Australian born: some doctors; some lawyers; some teachers; the majority were far more educated that those in authority.

John was particularly offended by this term, as it referred to a drifter, a hobo, a bum, without employment, or business, or even purpose. It was a word commonly used to refer to thieves and pirates. John was no pirate, nor hobo, or bum, and had paid his own way on every occasion, taking from no man or government. But yet the government, including the governor himself, referred to John and his mates alike as 'vagabonds'.

With the burgeoning trade and influx of migrants, Governor Charles La Trobe was frankly out his depth. To keep his public servants from resigning and turning their hand to mining, he was forced to offer a fifty percent increase to their wages. To pay for this increase, he had to charge exorbitant licence fees, whether or not they found gold, instead of a gold duty tax payable only on the actual gold extracted.

By the time John had arrived in December 1852 La Trobe had already submitted his resignation. He had no care for the Victorian Colony. He was merely caretaking in eager anticipation of his replacement.

Dalton's Gold
By Peter D Matthews

He employed a Gold Commissioner for each goldfield, and paid them a whopping five hundred pounds per year, to enforce the payment of licence fees.

Then there was an Assistant Commissioner; a Police Inspector; followed by Mounted Police or 'Troopers', who were paid three shillings a day; and Police on foot or 'Traps' who were paid two shillings and nine pence per day; and don't forget the Aboriginal Police, also paid one shilling and a halfpenny per day.

Yet miners had to pay a licence fee of thirty shillings each month to renew their licence, which was in fact a tax. The offensive element of this fee, was the fee had to be paid whether or not they had found any gold.

As many of the Police left to become miners or pastoralists, and the population grew out of control, the government sought out men they could to enlist as police, purely for the enforcement of taxes. The vast majority of these critters were no more than uneducated, untrained, brutal thugs, called 'blue-pissants', referring to their despicable, argumentative, insignificant type with a big attitude to boot.

More than eighty percent of Van Diemen's Land (Tasmania) remained a penal colony. There were two equally atrocious places for secondary punishment: Port Arthur and the other Macquarie Harbour. Many of the convicts were there because of hideous crimes such as rape, murder, and bank or coach robbery. These

'Vandemonians' came over to Geelong, headed for Ballarat and were in turn enlisted as Police.

Many historians paint embellished pictures of Eureka being a force of Irish rebels, but in truth, the rebels were those enlisted by the government bureaucrats. Troopers and traps were sent amongst the goldfields with weapons and power which only turned them more brutal.

John had the misfortune of seeing firsthand what these blue-pissants were like.

One particular day, the sun was beating down with hardly a cloud in the sky, when John had just pulled up a bucket of soil from the hole. He was rocking the cradle to sieve for gold and he noticed a little beauty right there in front of him. It was laying on the sieve looking at him. It shone in the sunlight like a yellow sparking diamond, as if it were reaching out to John to spot it.

Right at that moment two blue-pissants marched up to John, growling 'licence, mate,' while pointing two rifles with bayonets at his abdomen. They were both tall, one well built like a prize fighter, and the other thin and gangly but none the less sadistic.

John politely replied, 'I'll get it for you' as he walked towards his licence. It laid only a few feet away with his towel, shirt, waistcoat, coins, and his eighteen carat gold pocket watch with gold chain. The chain secured the watch to his front waistcoat pocket.

When he took his first step to his belongings, all of a sudden, one of the rifles pulled back. Not noticing what was happening behind him, John had thought they were allowing him to retrieve his licence, but instead he was hit from behind on the back of the head with the butt of a rifle. He was instantly knocked unconscious to the ground.

    The blue-pissants dragged John's unconscious body onto a cart, taking with them his belongings back to the police camp. John's mates realized and came running from all around to defend him from these violent brutes.

    Raffaello Carboni and a dozen of his mates ran all the way to the camp behind the cart. One fine gentleman ran for Dr Carr, who immediately raced to the police camp, with Margaret in toe. The diggers were held back by police from entering the camp.

    Dr Carr arrived just as the blue-pissants were dragging John's lifeless body off the back of their cart. Dr Carr insisted, 'Let me through. This is the future husband of my niece. Let me attend to his wounds.'

    Dr Carr, with Margaret aiding as his assistant, laid John's motionless body on an old table of rough slabs of timber. John was still unconscious, with blood pouring down the back of his head, flowing onto his shoulders. Dr Carr found a huge cut to back of his head, and began shaving and stitching to fix him up. Margaret was overtaken with grief, and held John close, gently sobbing while kissing his face. John woke up just as Dr Carr was finishing, seeing who was over him. His lips came to life as she kissed him. His lips met hers, and his

Dalton's Gold
By Peter D Matthews

arms rose up and embraced her like there was no tomorrow.

Dr Carr pulled Margaret back off John, allowing him to rise, and he gathered his belongings that lay by his side.

A licence, a shirt, a waistcoat with the right front pocket torn out. There was no watch, no coins - he had been pillaged by the local police, all in the name of justice in supposedly upholding the law.

John and Dr Carr were outraged. Dr Carr spoke aside with the Gold Commissioner but still within sight and earshot of John. The Gold Commissioner brought the officer concerned before him and enquired of John's money and watch.

The officer boomed out for all to hear as well as the Commissioner, 'Dearest Sir, there were no such items on his person'.

John noticed in the corner of his eye, his gold chain for his pocket watch, hanging out of the officer's pocket.

John piped up, 'There it is in your pocket'.

Dr Carr insisted he remove it from his pocket. The officer pulled the pocket watch out, only to find a broken link on the end where it had been forcibly torn out of John's waistcoat.

John exclaiming, 'There you go, this blue-pissant is a thief. That's my pocket watch, and there you go, the link is broken from being torn out of my waistcoat.'

Dalton's Gold
By Peter D Matthews

The officer quickly returned, 'This is my pocket watch, and was dislodged by your struggle, when I asked to see your licence'.

With a dozen stitches in the back of his head, John was in no fit state for a fight, but staggered to his feet saying, 'Let me have this stinking, lying, Vandemonian. He came up to me, demanding my licence at the point of bayonet, and in a good manner, I leant down to pick up my licence, and suddenly I was hit on the back of the head. All in the name of justice - I was robbed by this Vandemonian.'

The officer came close to talk with the Gold Commissioner and John could not quite hear what was being said, but what he saw disgusted him no end.

The officer pulled out of his pocket a small but brilliant gold nugget that glimmered like a diamond. It was the same nugget that John saw on the cradle just before the blue-pissants had turned up.

The Vandemonian slid the nugget into the hand of the Gold Commissioner, so that nobody could see. However he didn't realize that he did it in full view of John.

The Gold Commissioner tucked it safely away in his own jacket pocket, without a word. John said nothing more in fear. He might have just awoken, but he was not that drowsy to understand that if he accused the Gold Commissioner of corruption, he would be carted off and charged with treason.

Dr Carr not aware of what just transpired. He began to negotiate John's freedom with the Gold

Commissioner on the basis that due to the circumstances it may have been a misunderstanding. After all John was in good faith reaching for his licence, but may have been attacked by the officer 'inadvertently' in doing his duty.

The Gold Commissioner upon seeing the gathering of miners at the entrance to the police camp, decided to release John on the basis that he retracted his complaint of being robbed, as John's belongings may have merely been left behind at his camp. After all, he had a nasty knock to the head.

John knew that it was his gold pocket watch, and the Gold Commissioner had colluded with the officer to rob John of his wealth, but couldn't do anything about it.

Dr Carr went his way, leaving Margaret to stay with John and care for him that night. His mates helped John by lifting his arms over their shoulders, one on each side, taking the weight so that he could walk with them, which was about two miles back to their camp.

Many an incident happened on the goldfields. Miners being robbed by blue pissants were a regular occurrence, especially while they were taking their spoils to the gold sellers. It was the general feeling amongst the miners that the Gold Commissioner intentionally hired ex-convict Vandemonians to rob and pillage from the diggers. Was it not enough that they robbed the diggers with the taxes, that they violently robbed them of all of what was left?

Dalton's Gold
By Peter D Matthews

Many of the diggers were forced to arm themselves before carting off their gold to the gold sellers, so as not to be plundered by ruthless, murderess, thieving Vandemonians along the way.

Margaret stayed the night at John's camp to bathe his wounds. John was so excited to have Margaret come stay with him. His love, his future bride, was right there in his tent tending his wounds. He so much wanted to take her into his bed and ravish her with affection, yet restrained himself as a devout Catholic, waiting in anticipation for their wedding night.

Margaret slept in John's bed, and Carboni let John sleep on his. John's mates had made sure that John's glass was full of whiskey to help reduce the pain and give him some sleep.

Bewildered and dismayed, John searched his own soul that night, questioning whether he should stay at Ballarat or move on. He wondered whether Margaret would go with him, thinking she would, but only with Dr Carr's blessing. John toiled all night long. Come morning, somehow he just couldn't leave his mates behind. The diggers of Ballarat had somehow become his family and he just couldn't desert them.

While recovering, he spent the next few days walking the goldfields, looking for where he might lay claim next. He pondered his future, considering whether he should continue mining or go back to boot making.

He walked down Canadian Gully further onto a sandy flat area of ground. He noticed flickers of alluvial

Dalton's Gold
By Peter D Matthews

gold dust right to the surface. Was this the discovery he had dreamt of?

'Dalton's flat' was aptly named in honour of John Thomas Dalton.

3
DALTON'S FLAT

John raced back to his camp, excitedly gathering his belongings. Seeing what was going on, Carboni turned to John enquiring of him, 'What are you doing? Are you leaving?'

John whispered quietly, 'I found a flat with alluvial gold right to the surface. I think this might be the big one I've been waiting for. I'm moving camp.'

Carboni thought John was mad, shaking his head at him as a fool. John turned to a group of his mates, hoping to find someone who would take him seriously.

John excitedly blurted, 'I think I've found the pot of gold that I've been waiting for. At the end of the gully there is a flat with alluvial gold right to the surface.'

The Scobie brothers both laughed uncontrollably at John's expense. James jested, 'You're three parts full already and it's not even noon. What are ya drinking?'

John indignantly scoffed, 'No, I haven't been drinking. I'm telling you what I have just found.'

James Lyons and John Henry overheard the conversation. They seemed to take John seriously.

Dalton's Gold
By Peter D Matthews

Henry was standoffish, but Lyons said, 'Well Dalton, don't be dilly dallying around here, go and stake your claim'.

John gathered up all of his belongings and took off to stake his claim.

His head pounding and heart racing as he grabbed his pick, shovel, pale, panning bowl, and headed back to Dalton's Flat.

John frantically started digging, and before long he had one nugget, then two, then three...

They were all small but John was quietly excited and his spirits lifted. He was hopeful of what he might find next.

He thought to himself, 'I have found it. Eureka! This is the hole I have been waiting for.'

He raced back to his mates, showing them his three small but high quality gold nuggets, all of which were found in the first two feet from the surface.

Noticing John's excitement at his find, they decided to take a look. Carboni, Scobie, Lyons, and Henry grabbed a pick and shovel, and headed back with John to Dalton's Flat.

John's Irish born mate Peter Lalor overheard his conversation while selling grog to neighbouring miners, and decided to tag along.

Lalor was an experienced miner, having sunk deep shafts in search of high quality seams of buried gold up to one hundred feet on Eureka. John invited Peter's keen eye as Peter was a qualified civil engineer by profession.

Dalton's Gold
By Peter D Matthews

Peter was held in high esteem by the Irish born diggers as his father, Patrick Lalor, pushed for Irish freedom as the sitting member for Queen's County in the House of Commons.

Peter was a bit of an entrepreneur. He was not only a digger but also merchant and sly grog seller. The government banned alcohol on the diggings for some time, so Peter brought in grog selling it for one pound ten shillings when the normal price was about eight shillings a bottle. His services were greatly appreciated by the group of thirsty diggers on the goldfields, especially John and his mates.

Lalor's demeanour demanded respect, some six feet one and a half inches tall. He was rather good looking with a long face that seldom smiled, yet he possessed a rather cheerful temperament. He had dark brown hair, with dark brown long sideburns, and no moustache. His large flattened nose looked as if he had seen many scuffles as a child.

Peter Lalor was a straight fellow, completely trustworthy, despite what people might say. If you knew him well, and he believed in you, he would stand by you and fight with you unto the death. He was the embodiment of a real mate.

John staked his claim on Dalton's Flat. His mates were astounded to see gold dust on the surface which was relatively untouched, just as John had told them.

Lalor leaned over, examining the dust, rubbing the yellow glistening soil between his fingers. In a matter of fact voice he informed, 'Dalton, I think you are on to something here. Let's take a few blows and see what we find.'

Carboni grabbed a pick and started to swing, dragging the soil up like a plough. Up came small fragments of gold, clearly seen by the eye even without washing and panning.

Lalor said, 'If there is this much on the surface, the chances are that John's elusive nugget might well be here'.

Carboni excitedly jumped for joy, asking, 'How about we all go in together John? We work digging the shaft down in turns and whatever we find, we split up equally.'

John said, 'That's fine by me, if it's fine with all of you'.

Lalor took the initiative to get started, saying, 'I can get my hands on anything you need. Come on boys give me a hand to lug the timbers down, while Dalton and Carboni start digging.'

All agreed so John Dalton and Carboni started digging down as far as they could until shoring was required. The others gathered slabs, ropes, sperm candles, buckets and John's cradle.

Carboni and Dalton worked tirelessly until just before nightfall, benching the hole ready for shoring timbers at dawn. As the darkness fell and exhaustion set in, with no time left to set up John's new camp, they made a fire and all slept around it that first night on Dalton's Flat. They sat around the fire together, with a

Dalton's Gold
By Peter D Matthews

billy of tea, a leg of mutton, and Lalor brought a loaf of fresh bread from the baker.

'That hit the spot. What about a whiskey or three to wash that down' John exclaimed.

Carboni piped up, 'Lalor's shout, since we dug the hole'.

Lalor being an obliging fellow smiled and pulled out a fresh bottle of whiskey, that he had tucked away in his back pocket already prepared. John just smiled as they sat around the fire that night, contented with his find, waiting in eager anticipation for dawn.

The next morning they all arose to a thick mist just before daylight. They started the day around the camp fire again with a digger's breakfast of chops, bread and tea. Then it was off to a hard day's work once again.

Having broken through the alluvial crust, finding about twelve troy ounces so far, Lalor jumped in examining the soil in readiness to shore up the water sodden unstable shaft. This time they were in pursuit of the deep leads, and needed his expert help.

James Lyons pulled together the puddle clay and rammed it between the slabs of timber to try to hold back as much water as possible. John and his mates kept digging the shaft through this perdiferous material. At the end of day two and having risked their lives, they came up empty handed after a long gruelling day.

John and his mates sat around the camp fire that evening, again drinking away the pain of the day. The only person who profited that day was Peter Lalor from liquor sales.

Dalton's Gold
By Peter D Matthews

Month by month they worked tirelessly, without much advancement, just making barely enough for food. We can only imagine what it would have been like. Yet they begrudgingly continued to pay the 'stinking licence fees', with little to show for it.

It had been over twelve months since the two large finds in Canadian Gully. Many a miner had pulled out, and John wondered whether to do the same.

With Governor La Trobe's resignation, John and all his mates looked forward in anticipation to the arrival of the new Governor. Sir Charles Hotham arrived in Victoria in June of 1854.

Hotham was an experienced naval commander. He was appointed by the Duke of Newcastle to bring 'responsible government'. Rather than fulfilling Hotham's request for a ship, he was given the post to reform the Victorian Colony.

Realizing the state of the public purse, Hotham immediately ordered Gold Commissioner Rede to enforce collections with twice monthly licence hunts. These hunts were no different to fox hunting in England, but instead with Australian immigrants as their prey.

One such hunt brought blue-pissants crawling down every hole in search of diggers without a current licence. John heard they were coming so went up to pay his licence fee.

John stood waiting for hours in the sun for the officer to take his licence fee. He waited in line behind a timber rail. The indignation got too much for John. He had refrained for far too long, and couldn't hold his water any longer. As was the custom, he mistook the licence office tent for the toilet.

On his return from the government camp, he was asked to see his licence four times by the blue-pissants. He saw another digger running down the gully away from a trooper, when all of sudden John heard the 'crack' of a firearm and raced to the scene. He found a fellow digger laid prostrate with his face in the muck. John noticed the digger had been shot in the back, right between the shoulder blades. He turned him over but found he was already dead.

As the trooper approached, 'You're next, if you run. You're licence mate', he barked at John.

John was horrified at the treatment, but produced his licence for the fifth time. He had no choice but bite his tongue in fear of his life.

Another mate was dragged off without a licence. He was fined five pound by the magistrate with two and a half pound given to the arresting officer.

Needless to say this became quite a lucrative sport for ruthless vandemonians, much to the disgust of the honest digger.

It was about five o'clock in the afternoon on 26th August 1854 that Governor Hotham along with Lady Hotham descended upon the camp. They visited the gravel pits with over five hundred blue-pissants in toe.

John and his mates gathered around for Governor Hotham's address to the diggers.

Articulately he announced, 'Diggers, I am delighted by your reception. I will not neglect your interests and welfare. Thank you.'

His short and simple speech gave some reassurance to the diggers, although it proved to be just words. A hunt began the next day and continued from that time onwards, twice a week.

Eureka on Dalton's Flat

It was the 8th of September 1854. John was digging down sixty feet below the surface on Dalton's Flat, when 'chink' was the noise from his pick.

John excitedly pulled out the pick for a second blow. To his amazement, it stuck in, but he couldn't remove it. Lyons above lowered down a second pick for John to uncover his find.

John carefully dug around a quartz boulder exposing a huge glistening yellow nugget. His excitement turned into jubilation as he yelled, 'Eureka. I have found you', talking to his new found nugget.

The nugget was at least ninety-five per cent or twenty-three carat pure gold, weighing 1177 troy oz (36.61kg). In today's market this one nugget was worth about $1,900,000 Australian Dollars.

While removing the gold nugget, John was astounded to see so much yellow glistening under the light of the sperm candle.

John tied a rope around the gold nugget and Lyons pulled it up out of the hole, closely followed by John Dalton. In his jubilation, he ran with the nugget under his right arm all the way to the hospital to show his find to Margaret and Dr Carr.

Arriving at the hospital, he ran into Dr Carr, dropping his gold nugget on the table. Proud and excited, he insisted 'I have found my fortune. Here it is. This is one of the largest gold nuggets ever found here at Ballarat. Now, I can marry your niece?'

'Certainly lad, you surely can' replied Dr Carr as he turned to Margaret.

Margaret leaped into the arms of John, and kissed him passionately on the lips.

John was beside himself. All of his dreams had come at once. Then he realized he had taken off with the nugget without even thinking of his mates.

Overcome with emotion, John blurted, 'I'll have to get back to tell the rest of my mates, but I'll be back later for you Margaret'.

John picked up his nugget and headed back to the camp. On his way back, many of his mates stopped him, congratulating him on his find.

Meanwhile he noticed Dr Carr heading into the Gold Commissioner's tent, which he thought was a bit unusual.

Arriving back at the camp, he broke open a bottle of whiskey to share with his mates. Just then a dozen troopers rode up.

'Are you John Dalton' asked the armed trooper.

John replied hesitantly, 'Yes. What do you want with me?'

Dalton's Gold
By Peter D Matthews

'Rede has requested your presence' replied the Trooper in a soft and welcoming voice.

The Vandemonian on foot standing by the side of the trooper insisted, 'Bring your gold nugget with you'.

John thought Dr Carr had spoken to Rede, merely being proud to announce that it was his niece's fiancé who found the nugget. John walked to the government camp without question with the police, expecting accolades and protection for his gold.

John walked into the Commissioner's tent. The pretentious Commissioner Robert Rede sat on a rich red leather armchair, behind a hand-carved wooden desk with a red leather inlay in the surface.

'Like a whiskey, Dalton?' he said, while pouring from his decanter into two glasses.

'That would be nice' John replied, thinking this was a better way to be treated than the previous times in the government camp.

'May I have a look at your nugget' Rede asked. Not that John had much choice, but replied 'Yes, why not', placing it on the desk.

Rede looked over the nugget with a large magnifying glass. 'It's a real beauty' he exclaimed, before asking, 'Have you got your licence on you by chance.'

John reached into his back pocket and realised he had left it at his camp. He said, 'No Sir. I have finished work for the day. I left my licence at the camp, where your officers brought me from.'

Dalton's Gold
By Peter D Matthews

Rede hesitated for a moment, puffing on his cigar. He swigged another mouth full of whiskey before shrewdly replying, 'Well, we have an interesting predicament indeed. I have a gold nugget on my desk taken from the goldfields of the crown, and you have no licence on you to confirm that you're entitled to remove such gold.'

John indignantly insisted, 'You know very well I had my licence on me at the time of removing this nugget. I brought it back to my camp to show my mates, and your blue-pissants dragged me here under false pretences. The gold belongs to me and my mates. I saw what you did last time, stealing my gold after I was hit on the back of the head. Now you want to be such a blatant thief as to try to steal it from me in front of everyone.'

John just couldn't help himself. He blurted it out before ever thinking. It was too late - he couldn't put it back into his mouth.

Grabbing his sword, Rede thrust it to John's throat. In a threatening, almost growling voice, he uttered, 'Careful young Dalton, for I have the power to cut you down right here. I will not be called a thief. I have promised the first big nugget to the Governor for the Lady Hotham.'

Rede eased his sword away from John's throat, allowing him to speak.

'I don't care for your promises to the Governor. This gold is ours' John forthrightly insisted.

Rede paced the floor in silence for a long nervous whole minute. With a rather cunning look upon his face, just like a crocodile smiles before he strikes, Rede suggested, 'Dalton, if you would donate this nugget in honour of our Governor, I will not run you in for not holding a licence, nor for treason in questioning the integrity of a senior government official. For that, the punishment is certain death. You will be allowed free licence fees from this date forth. The nugget will be named, "The Lady Hotham", and you will have the right to continue digging.'

John was reviled by Gold Commissioner Rede's actions, He questioned, 'How could you steal from us? You are a disgrace. How could when you used to be a digger?'

Rede completely ignored John's comments like water off a duck's back. Instead he returned, 'The alternative is being run in and your gold seized, and you carted off to Hotham to be hanged. Would you rather that?'

Rede hesitated for a moment, before suggesting 'To save face you may tell your digger mates that your licence was not up to date, therefore the gold belongs to the crown, and will be given to Lady Hotham'.

John begrudgingly agreed. He chose to be a pauper rather than a convict. He had no desire at twenty-four to be hung on the gallows of Melbourne's prison, or at best be taken off to a Vandemonian prison.

Dalton's Gold
By Peter D Matthews

'Well, Dalton, you are free to go then. I will be sure to let Lady Hotham know of your generosity' Rede snorted, with a distinctive snigger in his voice.

John was disgusted and infuriated as he walked out of the government camp. He was astounded that the Australian Government could be so corrupt.

Walking past the blue-pissants and red-toads at the entrance to the camp, they laughed violently at him. One trooper yelled out, 'Got your licence, whacker?'

John just looked at him with a stare, knowing full well the insulting trooper was calling him a dickhead to his face, but there was little he could do. He wanted to shoot him in the chest or slam him to the ground.

One filthy Vandemonian unzipped his fly front trousers just as John walked past, but John didn't notice. All of sudden he reached into his trousers and pulled out his 'old wrinkled fella', and urinated on John's left leg.

'That's it' John yelled.

He turned ninety degrees in a fraction of a second, and thrust his right fist straight into the nose of the unsuspecting Vandemonian. He dropped him to the ground. Blue-pissants came from everywhere around, grabbing John, trying to drag him to the ground. He dropped two more before they managed to subdue him, but it took no less than a dozen men.

Rede came out screaming, 'Throw him in the lock-up. He can stay there a while until he cools down. In the morning he can decide whether he goes back to his camp or off to Hotham.'

Dalton's Gold
By Peter D Matthews

The pissants dragged John to the lock-up. It was a filthy rat infested hole that was not even fit for pigs. John sat in the corner contemplating his decision while fending off rats all night long.

It was a long dreadful night in the lock-up. But it did give John some time to think things over. He remembered seeing Dr Carr go into the government camp as soon as John left with his nugget. Dr Carr, although Margaret's' uncle, was no doubt a government spy and was allowed to stay in the hospital as a partner as long as he spied on the diggers.

But to do that to John and ultimately his own niece, was unforgiveable in John's eyes. He decided to say nothing and wait for the right moment for his revenge. John knew the perfect moment would eventually come, and all he had to do was wait.

He reminisced of being back on the diggings in the bottom of the hole. He remembered seeing glistening gold under the light of the sperm candle. He thought, 'Maybe this nugget was only one of many in the hole, or maybe even small in comparison to what I might find below'.

John pondered his future and that of his future bride. Finally after two years since they departed the ship, John was about to be given Margaret's hand in marriage. He may be able to turn his back on the goldfields, but not on Margaret.

Come morning, Rede and a dozen of his animals came to the lock-up. Rede inquired, 'Well Dalton, have you made a decision? Are you going back to your camp or am I going to send you on to Hotham?'

John didn't want to show his anger that burned inside, so strategically replied in a fearfully lowly voice, 'Yes Sir, I would like to go back to my camp.'

Rede gleefully replied, 'I'm glad you've come to your senses. But remember our agreement. You break that agreement and I will hunt you down, and dismember your body, leaving a piece of you at every corner of this town for all to see what happens if you betray me.'

'Release him' Rede ordered. The blue-pissant who urinated on John was there with white tape over his nose and dried blood all over his bruised face.

After walking out of the large iron gate entrance of the camp, John tuned to the blue-pissant saying 'You look like you ran into a wall last night. You'll have to be more careful. Maybe you shouldn't drink so much, then you wouldn't be running into walls or urinating on yourself.'

John felt a crack to the back of the head by another blue-pissant, but John thought it was well worth the pain as he couldn't resist blurting out his wise crack.

John walked back to his camp on Dalton's Flat. He was dirty and covered in bruises, but within him rose a spirit of righteous anger, turning his former fear into a desire for justice and reform.

4
SECRET GOLD

John walked upright with his shoulders back, not looking left or right. His face was stern with every muscle tense as he walked through town. Every digger he passed just looked at him, giving him plenty of room to walk by. They all knew that look and dare not say a word. It was a look of anger, burgeoning upon a murderous rage.

As he arrived back at his camp, Margaret was waiting for him to arrive. She spent the night wondering what had happened to him.

'I have breakfast for you, my love' Margaret said in a sweet innocent voice. She had no idea what horrendous treatment he had endured in the past twelve hours.

Immediately John's heart melted, realizing his folly. The reason he came to Ballarat was after his sweetheart, Margaret.

He had found gold, but was robbed. He had found a new land, and loved it. More importantly, he had fallen head over heels in love with little Margaret Carr.

Margaret had asked her aunt for some provisions to make them both breakfast. She prepared a royal feast for John, thinking he had found gold, and was now to be her long awaited husband.

She sat John down near the fire. Margaret grabbed a towel, wet the end and added a couple of drops of scented oil, then began wiping John's brow.

John sat there amazed, just watching and receiving her love, not saying a word. His eyes were clearly fixed on her every move. His broken heart, crushed of betrayal, was soon forgotten as she cleaned him up for breakfast.

Margaret served John four rashers of bacon, two lamb chops, and two fresh duck eggs, finished with a slice of fresh bread, hand toasted over the camp fire with her finest handmade orange marmalade.

This was the staple diet of the English and those in government employ, and Margaret was used to cooking for Dr Carr every morning for breakfast.

John's mates sat back out of the way drooling over John's breakfast, allowing him to have breakfast uninterrupted with his future bride. They too were not aware of what transpired the night before, but couldn't understand why he didn't come back with the gold nugget.

They all thought he had spent the night celebrating at a hotel with Rede and other government officials. But yet he arrived back dirty, as if he had been in a fist fight in the street.

His mates dare not interrupt. After all if they tried to pull John away from Margaret - it was not going to be a good day!

As John sat with a cup of tea and his future bride around the campfire, his brazen mate Peter Lalor strode up.

Peter inquired of John, 'I trust you have our nugget safe. Are you ready to go and find another one even larger today?'

John didn't want to talk in front of Margaret. Instead he insisted, 'I'll talk to you down the hole as we work. We don't have time to sit and chat. Let's get moving.'

At that John rose and kissed Margaret appreciatively saying, 'Thank you so much my love - that was delicious. And it was wonderful to see you. I must go, but I will be back at dinner time if you are still here?'

Margaret said, 'I'll be here for you. I'll prepare your dinner. If you are going to be my husband, you will need to see that I can cook.'

John chuckled, 'I'd marry you even if you couldn't cook. I'd cook for you, my love.'

She smiled at John as he walked off towards the hole with his mates.

To stop claim jumpers, James Lyons slept at the top of the hole all night with a rifle. News of John's find spread fast and people came from everywhere, almost on top of John's claim.

Dalton's Gold
By Peter D Matthews

John asked his mates to huddle close so he could tell them what happened last night. He apologetically, but optimistically averred, 'My friends and partners, the nugget we found yesterday is gone. It was taken by Rede for Lady Hotham. They brought me on false pretences to their camp, and as I didn't have my licence on my person, they stripped me of our gold.'

The faces of his mates changed, but John continued, 'However, what I didn't tell them is the nugget was only one of many nuggets in this here hole. Let's allow this one to slide, but no more do we tell anyone of our finds, apart from us here present. We will take our share at the end of each day, sell it or keep it in our money belts, or bury it under our tents. We tell nobody, then we can't be ripped off again.'

Although each one was livid, all agreed they could do nothing but move on.

John climbed down into the hole while the others stayed on the surface. John shovelled dirt into the bucket. It was hoisted by James Lyons using a rope behind a horse to pull the bucket up to the surface.

Carboni manned the cradle in the creek bed with the others carting the soil back down to Carboni at the creek. Fortunately at Dalton's Flat the trickling creek was not far away from the hole.

The soil was tipped into tubs of water and washed up to three times, then tipped into the cradle. The cradle was rocked furiously to separate the larger nuggets and the remainder of fine gold flowed through

Dalton's Gold
By Peter D Matthews

the metal sieve into a water hole. The fine gold in the water hole was also collected - this was the gold dust.

Nugget after nugget was pulled out of that hole, but no cries of 'Eureka' were shouted as before. A shout from another hole down further allowed the attention to shift. All the while John and his mates were silently making a fortune.

Dinner time came about noon. Carboni stayed to protect the hole, while John and his mates went off to their camps.

Margaret was there just as she promised.

As John walked towards the camp, all he could smell was an overwhelming rich aroma of Margaret's' cooking. He thought, 'I must be the luckiest man alive'.

'What's for dinner, my love? I am starving. Something smells wonderful' John expressed as he approached the campfire.

Margaret replied, 'I found your left over mutton so decided to make you my famous Irish stew. I hope you like it?'

John sat down by the fire. Margaret wiped his face and hands with a towel, just as she did earlier that morning.

'Here you go, my love. Tell me what you think?' Margaret said as she waited with baited breathe to hear.

John's mother used to make Irish stew with mutton back home, so he was well accustomed to it. In fact it was one of his favourites.

Dalton's Gold
By Peter D Matthews

He sat back eating Margaret's stew, soaking it up with the remainder of the fresh loaf of bread from breakfast.

The aroma from Margaret's Irish stew captivated him as he lifted the spoon to his mouth. The taste was rich and smooth, nothing quite like he knew - it was so much better than his mother's!

John chuckled looking over at Margaret saying, 'Irish stew was one of my mother's specialities, and one of my favourites growing up. Yet this is so much better than my mother's. Where did you learn to cook like that?'

Margaret giggled in an appreciative tone, 'My mother taught me how to cook. She worked as a cook and I helped her in the kitchen. She taught me everything I know.'

John had no idea that Margaret was actually a cook and a nurse.

John acknowledged, 'What a blessed man I am. I have found my fortune. I have found a wonderful place to live. But most importantly, I have found not only a beautiful wife but she is an unbelievably good cook. Could it get any better?'

Margaret sat there sweetly with a big smile, fluttering her eye lids at John.

After dinner John and his mates went back to work the hole. Over the next few days they worked quietly and tirelessly, seemingly with no real outcome. But secretly they had stumbled upon a full cubic metre of small gold nuggets. Any large finds were put directly into a hessian sack, and not taken up with the soil. That way others around thought there was little to report.

At the end of that long painstaking day, John climbed out of the hole, dragging with him a full sack of gold nuggets. Carboni also had a hessian sack down near the water hole but in it were only a few small nuggets to disguise the catch of the day.

Over the following days they carefully removed 2,640 troy oz (82.113kg) of similar quality gold to 'The Lady Hotham' nugget. This equates to roughly $4.2M Australian dollars in today's market, split six ways.

'The Lady Hotham' nugget was never seen again by John. It was taken by the red-toads directly to Lady Hotham that very evening that Rede stole it from John Dalton. It is expected that Lady Hotham had it melted down and fashioned into her own personalised jewellery.

Rede seemed to think this would buy him favour with Hotham, but in fact it reinforced Hotham's already misled convictions that the miners could afford the disproportionate tax. In turn Hotham ordered a crackdown on licence fee evasion.

John and his mates had removed an awful lot of gold from the hole. They had dug down to just over one hundred feet, when it seemed to run dry. Peter Lalor said, 'Dalton, I think it's time to move on. Why not sell this hole now for a hundred guinea and go our separate ways. You've made enough here to live it up. So why not?'

John happily echoed, 'Sounds fine to me. I might have to spend some time at the Bath Hotel.'

Carboni agreed.

Lalor smiled, 'I know just the blokes to talk to. Instead of just walking away from the hole, let's sell it to them' pointing to a group of diggers nearby.

While gathering all of their tools, Lalor spoke with the neighbouring diggers. John could overhear him conceding, 'This was the lucky hole where "The Lady Hotham" was found and we have had a fight, so we're selling our claim for a hundred guinea. That is, if you're interested?'

Lalor came back with four men prepared to pay eighty guinea for the claim. John thought, 'after all, eighty guinea (eighty-four pound) was not bad for a depleted claim.'

That equated to almost an year's wage for the average man. Without hesitation John confirmed by a nod, as if he was upset at the amount, but in reality, he was elated.

The new owners benched the hole to 135 feet. They found small amounts of gold to cover the cost of purchasing the claim, but nothing to write home about.

Lalor headed back to the Eureka along with the Scobie brothers. James and George pitched their tent just behind the Eureka Hotel, for close access to the pub of course.

James Lyons and John Henry stayed on Dalton's Flat, staking another claim with a couple of their mates.

Dalton's Gold
By Peter D Matthews

They kept an eye on John's tent while he and Raffaello Carboni headed to the Bath Hotel.

With money in his pocket; gold in his belt; and of course kilos of gold buried under his tent; John had money to burn. The best hotel in town was the newly built Bath Hotel. It was the first sophisticated hotel built specifically for royalty and landed gentry in 1853, by Thomas Bath.

Thomas Bath was an English born Australian pioneer in his mid thirties, with long beard, balding head, large nose to which he looked down upon the diggers as the scum of the earth. After all, he was landed gentry from Cornwall, and John a detested Irish Canadian.

Raffaello Carboni by this time was a well respected linguist and poet. He managed to get through the door in his Sunday best. Carboni introduced John Dalton to Thomas Bath as a local landowner of Smythesdale, therefore John was accepted as gentry.

Coming from the goldfields and living in tents and bark huts, to stand before the magnificent recently completed Georgian timber hotel was a sight for sore eyes.

John was excited to enter the exclusive Bath Hotel. Its fine sawn timber deck was covered by a skillion verandah, leading directly into a magnificent timber staircase and open lounge bar.

John sat down on a dark red chesterfield leather armchair with numerous buttons. They were tailored specifically for the English nobles. Between his chair and

Carboni's chair was a Queen Anne style hand carved coffee table. The hotel was fitted out with nothing but the best.

This was all very new to John. Rather than fronting a bar to order, a waitress dressed in fine black with white lace soon arrived to take their order.

The very polite waitress offered, 'What can I get for you dear Sirs?'

Carboni ordered a glass of fine red wine, while John hollered, 'What type of drink to you keep? Do you have any American Bourbon?'

'Yes Sir' she warbled, 'We have Evan Williams Straight Kentucky Bourbon Whiskey, all the way from the America.'

'I will have a bottle of that. Thank you' John articulated in a rather distinguished voice.

'A bottle Sir? We normal sell by the glass' she scoffed. By her tone, it was apparent that she was questioning whether John could afford it.

John pulled out a fifty pound note, which was quite a lot of money in 1854. He placed it on the coffee table and forcefully grunted, 'I'll have a bottle, but by all means, you may serve it in a glass. I am thinking of staying a few days. Can you organise us two guest rooms upstairs?'

The rather embarrassed waitress ran off at once to get John his order while speaking to the owner, Thomas Bath Esquire.

Thomas Bath came over to talk to Dalton and Carboni. Turning to John, he graciously offered,

Dalton's Gold
By Peter D Matthews

'Welcome to my here Bath Hotel, dear Sirs. I believe you require two rooms.'

John took pleasure in mocking with a similar gracious accent, 'Yes, dear Sir, I would like to stay a few days in Ballarat, and I am considering this hotel for my upcoming wedding reception'.

'Indeed Sir, we will make your stay the most memorable stay at my here Bath Hotel. So much so, that you will remember it for the rest of your life' gestured Thomas Bath.

John contented, 'Thank you, dear Sir'. Hesitating for a moment with a puzzled look upon his face, John questioned, 'Could you do something for me?'

'Call me Thomas, dear Sir. How may I help?' he eagerly responded.

John requested, 'Can you send someone to the hospital for my fiancé and give her a note, and could you find a partner for my friend here, that we may dine together tonight?'

Thomas warmly accommodated, 'Certainly Sir. I will send someone immediately. What is her name, may I inquire?'

Proud as punch John instinctively offered, 'Margaret Carr, Dr Carr's niece. Do you know her?'

'Oh' Thomas sniffs in a rather condescending tone.

He continued, 'I know Dr Carr. He does frequent this hotel with certain government officials.' Thomas Bath realized John was taken aback by his impulsive disrespectful scoff at Dr Carr. Before John had time to respond, Thomas went on to say, 'But I am not familiar with your fiancé'.

John, being the larrikin and to lighten the mood, blurted 'Don't be concerned, Thomas. I don't like him either.'

Thomas sent one of his maids at once to Margaret. Arriving at the hospital, she pleaded, 'I am here to deliver a note to Miss Margaret Carr. Is she here?'

Margaret overhearing her conversation, piped up, 'I'm Margaret Carr?'

'Your fiancé has requested your presence for tea tonight at the Bath Hotel and asked me to give you this note' the maid happily boomed.

Margaret excitedly opened the note which read:
To my dearest Margaret, I am staying a
few nights in luxury at the Bath Hotel,
having made my fortune. Would you
please come and join me for tea tonight,
along with my dear friend Raffaello
Carboni.
I long to see your beautiful face, adorned
by your long dark flowing hair. Please join
me my dear, and we will enjoy a feast of
samples in preparation for our wedding
reception.

Margaret was overjoyed with the invitation as the Bath Hotel was known as the place to be, and she had never visited the Hotel before. To have her wedding reception at the Bath Hotel was beyond her wildest dreams.

Margaret sent message back that she would arrive at six o'clock that evening, and looked forward in eager anticipation of dining at the Bath Hotel with her future husband.

As soon as she finished her shift at the hospital, she raced back to her quarters to ready herself for her fiancé.

Carboni was introduced to Mary. She was a young red headed Irish girl, quietly spoken, but dressed in a sleek black dress that could seduce any man. She sat down next to Carboni and talked while they all waited for Margaret to arrive.

As John watched the doorway, a young lady appeared in a bright red silk dress. The dress was a little shorter than the rest, which was just not done in those days. I should note that this was her only formal dress that she brought from Ireland and was by this time a few years old, and really a little too small for her.

Her petite ankles were dressed in red shoes to match her dress, exposing her legs, just above the ankle. Her long dark hair was not tied in a bunn like most, but was allowed to flow freely, grabbing the attention of every man in the region.

As she walked towards John, he realized this gorgeous woman that approached was Margaret - his future bride. He stood and kissed her on the cheek. Then he pulled back a chair as a gentleman, and gestured 'You look absolutely stunning my love. I am glad you could come.'

Margaret excitedly whispered, 'I have wanted to come here since it was built. It is just magnificent. Can we afford the wedding reception here?'

John graciously asserted, 'For you my love, anything.'

Margaret didn't realize it, but John had also sent for Father Patrick Smyth, their local Catholic Priest.

Father Smyth arrived and they arranged the wedding before tea. It was settled. The wedding would be held at St Alipius Catholic Church on Monday 20th November 1854, and the reception afterwards at the Bath Hotel. It was the tradition to marry on a Monday after the Sabbath.

The date was set and they settled in for tea, when Dr Carr walked in to seat himself at a table near the entry with Commissioner Rede and two of his cohorts. Fortunately, they did not see John and Margaret seated in the corner to the rear.

John quietly whispered, 'Don't turn around quickly but look who has strolled in to sit with the Commissioner?'

Carboni whispered back, 'Devil! I told you he was a government spy.'

Margaret turned around slowly to see who they were talking about. She sat there stunned to see her uncle seated with Rede. 'A government spy?' she questioned. 'I would not have believed it, had I not seen it with my own eyes' Margaret panted.

Dalton's Gold
By Peter D Matthews

Just as she was watching, her uncle passed papers to Rede. Then Rede passed a clip of sterling notes back to Dr Carr.

John whispered to Margaret sincerely, 'My love, you know I love you more than anything, and I would never steer you wrong. I had no idea that he was coming here, but I did suspect he was a spy. Just after I left you at the hospital with my new found gold nugget, I saw your uncle running into the government camp. Within an hour or so Troopers showed up at my camp. I didn't give the Lady Hotham nugget as a gift, but it was taken from me by Rede for the Lady Hotham. It was your uncle who betrayed me.'

Margaret sat there bewildered for a moment thinking back, and suddenly realized that her uncle did run out of the room just after John left. Upon his return, Dr Carr did place a clip of sterling notes on the old wooden table before he sat down for a drink.

'It's true', she exclaimed. 'I saw him that night with another clip of money, just the same as I have just seen him take from the Commissioner before my very eyes' she gasped.

Margaret wanted to confront her uncle but John made her promise that she would not mention it as John feared a reprisal from Rede. With John's gentle idioms of reassurance, he promised to take care of her for the rest of her life, confirming she would never have to worry about her uncle again, Margaret slowly simmered back to her normal placid self.

'Leave him to God', John conceded, 'All in good time. The Lord will repay his treachery.'

She renounced the name of Carr, and muttered, 'I am ashamed and disgusted to be called a Carr. My name will now be Margaret Carry so that my future generations will never know of my former uncle, Dr Alfred Yates Carr.'

Instead John turned the conversation around to focus on enjoying a superb meal together in fine dining, with his mate Carboni, and Mary, his new found friend for the night.

Dalton & Carboni, mere miners from the muck, sat back in their stately seats, enjoying being served the finest the Victorian Colony had to offer.

Margaret demanded to stay with John. She had no desire to return to the hospital. John being a God fearing Catholic man paid for another room in the hotel for Margaret, under the name of Margaret Carry.

John stayed for a few days at the Bath Hotel. Margaret enjoyed it so much, that John let her stay there in the Bath Hotel until their wedding night.

Running short of funds, John walked back to his camp to dig up some more of his hidden gold, when all of a sudden a group of irritating blue-pissant troopers rode by. John knowing he didn't have his licence on him, crept around from the west into his camp on Dalton's Flat.

'Your licence, mate' John heard, just after he crawled into his tent. Upon producing his licence, the trooper galloped off in chase of another digger fleeing from the traps.

John gazed over to see one of his mates trip and be pounced upon by troopers and traps, only to come up in shackles with blood pouring down his face.

Nonetheless, the blue-pissants dragged him off to the lock-up for not paying the licence fee. John's blood almost boiled at the sight of his mate. The Australian born digger was dragged by his long blonde hair, face first through the dirt, leaving a trail of blood behind him.

John ran all the way back to the Bath Hotel to tell Carboni. Carboni and John realized their folly of enjoying indulging luxuries while their mates were still being brutalized by blue-pissants.

John and Raffaello set out for the lock-up to see their mate. As they arrived, they saw their mate being carried into the common lock-up area. He laid prostrate on the floor, hardly able to move, and covered in his own blood.

Raffaello yelled out to the blue-pissant guard, 'Excuse me, the fellow you have there in lock-up needs medical attention.'

'Piss off, mate. Otherwise I'll lock you up too' grunted the nonchalant Vandemonian.

John insisted to Carboni, 'I'll get Dr Carr and you get Peter Lalor.'

Hour after hour their pleas were ignored to release the digger to the hospital. Before long about two hundred diggers were protesting outside the government camp, which raised the attention of Commissioner Rede. After negotiations with Dr Carr, Rede released the digger to the hospital for treatment.

Two hours later the poor digger died in hospital from wounds to his head after a horrendous loss of blood. To this day nobody knew what happened to the digger because he died and couldn't tell his side of the story.

Rede inquired what happened from the trooper?

The trooper alleged, 'He fell and hit his head on a broken bottle while trying to escape arrest. I was just do'in my duty.'

But John knew different. Police pounced on this poor digger, bashing him within an inch of his life. His head was opened up, just the same as Dalton's head was opened with the butt of a rifle.

Without immediate medical attention the digger's blood poured out on the dirt of the common lock-up. By the time his body arrived at the hospital it was just too late. The unnamed digger was brutally murdered by police and left to die in gaol - but what for? He was being pursued for suspected tax evasion.

This brought great indignation amongst the diggers. The diggers were sick and tired of being fleeced, beaten and even killed, by those who were employed to uphold the law. These people were genuine hard-working Aussies with guts and determination - men and women of fortitude that could take no more.

5
QUELL THE DIGGERS INDIGNATION

    Hotham's answer to the miners indignation was another licence hunt, now every second day. His arrogant autocratic governing style alienated even his most loyal supporters, let alone John and his mates.

    Hotham continued his obnoxious hunts at the point of bayonet. Blue-pissants were smarming every hole hunting Aussie miners like foxes. They were treated worse than feral animals from the bush.

    John was perturbed by the agitation amongst his mates. He worked the shafts of Dalton's Flat in the morning, and spent the afternoons searching for a suitable home to bring up a family. The goldfields of Ballarat were such a treacherous place that he thought it was no place to start a family.

    He met up with his mate James Scobie along the way. Scobie and his old mate Peter Martin from

Scotland were heading up to the Eureka Hotel for a drink.

It was late Thursday afternoon 5th October 1854, when John decided to join them for a whiskey for 'Auld lang Syne' (old time's sake).

John didn't much like Peter Martin as he was a sly dog that couldn't be trusted. It was not that he was Scottish. He couldn't put his finger on it, but they seemed to be up to something. His old mate Scobie seemed to be taken in by Martin, who was known around the camp as a government spy.

John stayed for a few drinks but had to get back. John shook hands with James, who left John puzzled as he walked away.

James speculated, 'I may not see you again my old friend. I have to go away for a time. I have an offer I just couldn't refuse. You might hear things about me in the next few days, but I want you to know as my good mate, that none of them will be true.'

Peter Martin turned around and belted James across the face, shouting, 'shut up you drunken idiot. You are not allowed to say anything about it.'

At that Martin helped Scobie to his feet, concluding 'I think you have had far too much to drink. Time to get you to bed.'

John continued on his way, completely unaware of what was about to transpire in the next few days.

John had heard mining was taking off at Smythesdale which was only about 19km south west of Ballarat. This was also the place that Carboni told

Thomas Bath, of the Bath Hotel, that John was from. John in his curiosity decided to go and check out Smythesdale.

He rode out on horseback to Smythesdale the next day and stayed the night at the Smythesdale Hotel. He was pleasantly surprised by Smythesdale and rode back into Ballarat early on Sunday 8th October 1854 before the Sunday mass.

There was a frenzied crowd of people gathered outside the government camp, demanding truth and justice. Enquiring what the problem was, John was told, 'Your mate James Scobie has been murdered by James Bentley and his two thugs. Martin who was with him is still alive but severely beaten.'

Remembering the last thing James said to John when he left him at the Eureka Hotel, he decided to investigate further.

John ran over to Emmerson's Store, who were good mates with George and James Scobie. George Scobie with his portion of the gold from Dalton's Flat, bought a carting business bringing supplies from Geelong to Ballarat. One of his main clients was the Emmerson Store.

Phoebe Emmerson cynically reported, 'Apparently James was beaten to death. He was hit on the back of the head by someone behind the Eureka Hotel on Friday night. Most people seem to think it was James Bentley. George is away at Geelong, and they have no other family here that I am aware.'

John bellowed, 'I am as close to family that they have. I'll get to the bottom of this.'

John approached the entrance to the government camp and pushed through the crowd. He enquired with one of the guards, 'What happened to my mate, James Scobie?'

The blue-pissant completely ignored John. A protesting diggers nearby, yelled 'That bastard Bentley hit him over the back of the head, and killed him'.

'How do you know? Did anyone see what happened?' John asked.

'No, nobody saw nothing. T'was late at night. But he was with Martin. He was also hit over the head. Martin reckons it was Bentley and two of his blokes from the bar that jumped them' the digger boomed before returning to shout for 'justice'.

John headed off to the hospital, but was refused entry. He returned to the Bath Hotel where Margaret was waiting for him.

'Did you hear about James Scobie? she gasped. Margaret had nibbled her finger nails to the quick while waiting for John to return.

'Yeah I heard some garbled comment about be killed by Bentley. What did you hear?' John asked.

Margaret was a little frantic but matter-of-factly stated, 'All I know is James and this Martin fellow were out drinking. They knocked on the door of the Eureka Hotel after they were closed. Bentley told them to go away. Apparently, as they were leaving they smashed a window of the hotel. About 75 yards away from the hotel they were attacked by three men, leaving Martin injured, and James dead.'

'Have you seen his body' John asked.

'No I haven't. Actually someone must have done an autopsy and identified the body for the death certificate to be signed off. Normally that would be Uncle Alfred. Then he would give it to me to lodge with the registry office' Margaret acknowledged. She had worked in the hospital alongside her uncle for two years so knew the procedure down pat.

'I have already been there and they refused me entry. Can you get me in there?' John enquired.

'Surely can' Margaret declared.

Margaret took John back to the hospital and entered through the doctor's quarters. She enquired with the staff of Peter Martin, to find that no Peter Martin ever came to the hospital.

Margaret questioned, 'Where is the body of James Scobie'.

The nurse answered Margaret rather sheepishly, 'There is a drunken digger's body with an injury to the back of his head out the back. But you better hurry because they have sent for the undertaker to bury him. I think Dr Carr did say his name was Scobie.'

Margaret took John out to the back room where autopsies were performed and bodies were stored until the undertaker came. Morgues were not built in Victoria until the late 1850's. Until then, they were stored in hospital back rooms, and other public buildings.

Dalton's Gold
By Peter D Matthews

There was a body covered in a dry blood stained sheet laying on an old sturdy wooden table. As John approached he did not know what to expect.

'Was it his mate James Scobie?' he thought.

'Or was it someone else', but yet there was only one body in the back room.

'Was he hit on the back of the head?'

'Who really hit him on the back of the head?'

All these thoughts ran through John's mind as he approached the table. But the one thought that troubled him more than anything. That was what James had said the last time John spoke with him, where James speculated, 'I may not see you again my old friend. I have to go away for a time. I have an offer I just couldn't refuse. You might hear things about me in the next few days, but I want you to know as my good mate, that none of them will be true.'

'How could he know something was going to happen to him?' John pondered.

Did a plan backfire and his mate die - but yet Scobie asserted, 'None of them will be true'.

'What did he mean?' John thought.

Margaret carefully pulled back the sheet, exposing his head. The man was an older Irish looking fellow with a shaggy grey beard. As they rolled him over they confirmed this man was hit on the back of the head.

'But this is not Scobie or Martin' John pointed out.

Dalton's Gold
By Peter D Matthews

Placing the sheet back over, Margaret whispered, 'Someone's coming'.

Margaret grabbed John and hid in the corner behind archive shelving. It was Dr Carr and two other men.

They entered the room with a long timber casket, placing it on the floor. John and Margaret huddled into the corner trying to not make a sound. Dr Carr insisted, 'Give him some dignity. Keep him wrapped in the sheet.'

They picked up the body and placed it into the casket. One of the men had a timber carry-all with him, with tools in it. Out of it he grabbed a hammer and a hand full of nails. The undertaker nailed shut the top of the casket.

'Poor bugger, being hit over the head after being refused a drink' one of the undertakers remarked.

John soon realized that they thought this body was that of James Scobie, but John and Margaret knew this was not the case.

John and Margaret waited until Dr Carr and the undertakers had left, before creeping out of the back room. One their way through the Doctor's Quarters, in strode Dr Carr.

Margaret hopped from one foot to the other upon running into her uncle. She explained, 'We have come to see the body of John's mate, James Scobie'.

'Sorry you're too late. The undertakers have just taken him out' insisted Dr Carr.

Dalton's Gold
By Peter D Matthews

Margaret gruffly expressed, 'What sort of person are you? I trusted you, but yet you lie to my face. James Scobie was a friend of my here fiancé, and I knew him well. The man in that casket was not James Scobie.'

Dr Carr pulled them around the corner and out of plain view. He whispered, 'You'd better get out of here, and keep your trap shut. I don't want to have to be loading your body into another casket tomorrow.'

'Is that a threat?' John asked, as his face changed to a condescending stare of contempt.

'No laddy, you're in over your head already. Get out of here before one of Rede's men catches you in here asking questions about Scobie's body. Best you forget the name, James Scobie' announced Dr Carr.

John went off to mass with Margaret. After the mass John waited outside the Church for Peter Martin. Martin was nowhere to be found. John spent the afternoon looking through the entire camp, and there was no sign of Peter Martin or the real James Scobie.

'If the body was not James Scobie, then whose body was it?' John thought.

Monday came, and John sent Margaret back into the hospital to search for clues. She searched the records and found no death certificate signed for James Scobie. There was no autopsy report, nor any documents of any sort related to James Scobie.

'Hmmmm' they thought. This was all a bit odd.

Why would James Scobie foretell his death to John? It all seemed rather peculiar. Why was the man in the hospital portrayed as James Scobie when clearly it was not? Why would Dr Carr conspire to an alleged murder when the person may still be alive? Where was James Scobie? Where was Peter Martin for that matter?

Yet, Dr Carr ushered them out of the hospital, not wanting them involved, but at the same time implicated Commissioner Rede. Dr Carr was clearly in fear of his life. He was also concerned about John and Margaret opening their mouths. What was really going on? Did John really want to know? Could his own life really be in danger by asking questions?

The coroner's inquest was held the same day of Scobie's supposed death. The report published that the 'deceased died from injuries inflicted by persons unknown'.

Immediately the Bentley's were accused of killing James Scobie, but the unusual fact was that the body was not identified by anyone other than Dr Carr, who performed the autopsy. The Coroner did not know James Scobie, therefore could not personally identify the body. He relied on the testimony of the police and Dr Carr. Scobie's mate, Peter Martin had also disappeared.

The fact remains that the body buried was not James Scobie. There was no funeral - only a service held by George Scobie after arriving home to hear the news of his brother's death. There was no death certificate issued for James Scobie. Yet Scobie and Martin were nowhere to be found.

Peter Lalor and his mate John Phelan were furious, as were many of the diggers, believing that

Bentley was the murderer. The crowd were calling for Bentley's arrest. Everyone seemed to get caught up the moment and didn't even take the time to examine the evidence.

Nobody asked or even cared but merely wanted revenge, although upon an innocent family. The diggers had not carefully considered who James Bentley was, and what motive he may have had, or not had in this case. James Bentley was an ex-convict, come publican, and was the one on Eureka supplying the diggers booze.

Rede and his cohorts frequented the Bath Hotel along with the newly completely George Inn. These 'finer class' hotels were the image desired by Hotham, to draw a more upper class landed gentry to settle in the region.

The Bath Hotel opened in June 1853 followed by the Ballarat Inn within months, and then the George Inn in 1854. It stood opposite the government camp and overlooked the gravel pits.

The Eureka Hotel however was viewed by the government as a blight upon society. It was seen as the digger's meeting place - the cause of strife amongst diggers - the source of revelry to which they intended to stamp out.

John remembered overhearing a conversation while sitting in the Bath Hotel, where Thomas Bath questioned Rede, 'When are you going to deal with Bentley?'

He was sitting at a table just out of view, inside the rear doorway, along with Robert Milne the Sergeant

Major of Police. This was the same blue-pissant officer that John had seen his mate James Scobie with, along with another digger named Henry Goodenough.

'Very soon. You wait and see' Rede replied. John didn't think anything more of it at the time. Fortunately he was not noticed by Rede, as he tipped his hat on his way out to the gents to cover his face.

John thought at the time that Thomas Bath must have made some sort of complaint about opening hours of the Eureka Hotel. He did not even consider that they might have conspired to frame Bentley for murdering his mate.

John was recounting everything he had seen. He quickly came to the conclusion that something was very suspect. Rede wanted to shut down the Eureka Hotel and quell the diggers. But how was he going to accomplish this? Was it murdering an innocent man, parading him a James Scobie, to in turn frame Bentley?

James Bentley was arrested for the murder of James Scobie. Police Magistrate John D'Ewes acquitted James Bentley as there was no evidence to prove Bentley actually killed James Scobie. There was only hearsay, which surprised and angered Rede.

From that day onwards D'Ewes and Rede never saw eye to eye, and it appeared to John Dalton that Rede, 'Had it in for D'Ewes'.

The release of James Bentley brought mixed feeling around the camp. Some believed James Bentley was an innocent bystander but John knew this to be the case. Others such as Henry Goodenough, and fellow countrymen Thomas Kennedy, were rather vocal against the government. Really they did nothing more than stir up the masses.

John went to his mate Peter Lalor to try to tell him what he had seen, but unfortunately Peter was so overtaken by anger that he didn't even listen. He was too busy putting up placards calling for a public meeting.

6
TENSIONS RISE ON EUREKA

John attended the public meeting outside Betley's Hotel on 17th October 1854. It was a stinking hot and muggy day. It was time for a drink as far as John was concerned. Like John, most of the diggers attended the meeting for a drink, more than anything else. Nobody expected any sort of violent conflict.

As John approached the Hotel there were blue-pissants everywhere. They were inside the hotel, and gathered all around the outside of the hotel, facing the street like they were posted in positions to guard a fortress. Approaching in every direction was about 4,000 diggers who surrounded the hotel, all wondering the heck was going on.

The Eureka Hotel stood on the corner of Eureka and Bentley Streets, facing Eureka Street, Ballarat. To the right on Eureka Street was a bowling alley also owned by the Bentley's, then adjacent was the Linquist's Livery Stables.[1]

The timber two storey hotel had three bars, a billiards room, a games room, and several hotel rooms as sleeping quarters. The facade was rustic timber weatherboard which was overshadowed with three dormer windows above the second storey.

The blue-pissants had seized the hotel, and sent Bentley off to the government camp on horseback. The government provoked the diggers almost as if they wanted some sort of conflict. It was a standoff between the diggers and the blue-pissants. The diggers wanted justice, and the blue-pissants were posted at the hotel to suppress the diggers.

Tensions were burgeoning out of control when diggers were refused a drink at the bar. A fight broke out between blue-pissants and a number of diggers in the public bar. Meanwhile, troopers were galloping around and around, wildly circling the hotel. It seemed as if they were intentionally provoking the miners to act.

The well armed 40th regiment of red-coats marched in. They surrounded the rear of the hotel while the blue-pissants surrounded the front.

John stood back just watching and wondering what was about to take place. A number of his mates were thrown out of the hotel by force. Some started ripping boards off the side of the hotel in disgust. Others began throwing rocks and old boots at the blue-pissants.

Dalton's Gold
By Peter D Matthews

The bowling alley next door was a light timber framed building covered in canvas as a makeshift roof. A number of diggers, led by Henry Goodenough were carting in armfuls of paper, tar, and rags into the bowling alley and the rear of the hotel.

Just then Commissioner Rede rode in, taking all of the attention. He jumped off his horse and marched through the crowd up to the front window of the hotel. He tried to pacify the crowd, but they completely ignored him. He stood in the window to speak to the crowd, when an egg came flying through the crowd - a typical Australian gesture of disgust. It narrowly missed his face and hit the wall behind him, leaving egg yolk running down the wall.

Rede ordered the troopers to 'take the man in charge', but nobody seemed to know who was in charge. The disgruntlement was not restricted to one digger, but was widespread throughout the entire camp. Almost every person in the camp had been maltreated by the government at some stage.

The foot police continued fighting with diggers. Windows were smashed and all sorts of items were thrown out into the streets which frightening the horses. The troopers had no choice but back off and wait.

Rede seemed frustrated with a lack of action and ordered the military to go in, and throw everyone out of the hotel. Just as the military entered the hotel, John saw something sinister taking place.

Dalton's Gold
By Peter D Matthews

There was Henry Goodenough standing at the rear of the bowling alley with a rag on a stick. He soaked it in tar, then tipped it down into a nearby campfire. He lifted his blazing torch and ran towards the bowling alley, amidst the commotion of military intervention.

Goodenough lit the bowling alley alight, then headed towards the rear of the hotel. John ran towards Goodenough trying to stop him before he reached the hotel. Goodenough saw John running at him, and pulled out his .44 calibre colt dragoon revolver from his belt.

He pointed the pistol at John and fortunately John stopped in his tracks. John raised his hands in the air to signal his surrender. All John could do was pray that Goodenough didn't shoot him in the chest.

Goodenough saw John's surrender, and withdrew his weapon. Instead he ran and threw his fiery torch into the back corner of the hotel. The hotel was immediately ablaze, lit from the torch of Henry Goodenough.

'Why would he burn down the diggers drinking hole' John thought.

John's mind raced again, asking himself 'Why would a fellow digger point a pistol at me to stop me tackling him to the ground?'

'Was Rede's grandstand a distraction for what was happening to the rear. Was this a government plot? Was Goodenough a spy for the government? Was he even a miner?' John thought.

But Goodenough had been working amongst the diggers for months. It just didn't make sense to John at all.

John backed off, blending into the crowd and just watched at a distance. He didn't want to be shot down in cold blood by Goodenough.

A cry of 'fire' came from the crowd and within minutes the building was consumed. It was a flurry of activity as diggers removed everything of value, especially the plonk from the burning building. It was 'Bentley's shout' yelled a digger, as he handed out the bottles of warm porter wine and ale.

With black smoke billowing out of the rear of the hotel and bright orange flames rapidly spreading through the building, the red-toads backed out the hotel. Not wanting to risk their lives, they stood back at a distance, just laughing as they watched the hotel turn into burning embers. The insidious government personnel sat back in excitement as if they were in a London theatre watching a play. Fire seemed to excite the English. It disturbed John that the red-toads and blue-pissants took immense pleasure in watching the digger's water hole burn to the ground.

At that moment thunder cracked. The diggers were hoping for the skies to open. A hefty dark black cloud settled over the diggings but it the cloud didn't open for more than a few drops.

The Magistrate on duty, John Green, was there to read the riot act, if called upon by the Commissioner. But Green was also taken by the flames. He stood in awe and excitement, negating his duty of reading the riot act.

    The police along with military and government officials stood back watching the hotel burn, as if it were soothing to their soul. Or was it that they were satisfied with the conquest complete?

    With the hotel engulfed in flame and the dark clouds moved on, the wind picked up and raced through the building. It was levelling within half an hour from the time Henry Goodenough threw the blazing torch. Little was left but burning embers and ashes.

    John walked quietly amongst the crowd seeking out Goodenough. There he was standing around with the troopers in front of the fire with a bottle of porter's wine. He had a smile from ear to ear. He seemed proud as punch at his accomplishment.

    'Why would a miner be standing with troopers?' John asked himself. There is only one reason he concluded, 'He must be a spy feeding information back to government for money.'

    John headed back to Margaret at the Bath Hotel. On his way back he passed the government camp. He saw a ghost or was it his mate James Scobie? He was leaving the camp with a group of four troopers on horseback. John called out, 'James, is that you?' The man looked back to John, staring him in the face. He tipped his hat then turned back, riding off with two of the troopers. Two of the troopers turned towards John.

    'What da'ya want' a Vandemonian asked.

'Nothing Sir. I thought I had seen an old mate but I must have been mistaken' John said, in the hope of distancing himself from the real James Scobie who was riding away on horseback.

Fortunately the two troopers turned and rejoined Scobie. The four troopers continued with Scobie towards Melbourne. The unusual part is that James was a free man, yet he was on horseback accompanying the troopers. He was not in shackles as a prisoner. It didn't make much sense to John.

Dr Carr walked out of the camp and John said to him, 'I think I just saw my old mate Scobie'. He made this remark just to judge Dr Carr's response.

Dr Carr declared, 'Dalton you must be mistaken. I saw his body. He is dead and buried. As I said, keep your trap shut, and be on your way.'

John knew then that James Scobie was alive. He was taken as a free man by blue-pissants from Ballarat. This incident seemed to be from John's perspective some sort of government plot orchestrated by Rede, and no doubt Dr Carr was involved in some way.

John was filthy from being at the site of the fire, so he snuck in the back door of the hotel. He hid in fear of his life as he was one of few that knew what really happened with the burning of the Eureka Hotel. He was hoping that Goodenough didn't identify him to the troopers and they come looking for him.

A few days went by and John seemed safe but he was completely unaware of what happened in the camp during those few days.

Dalton's Gold
By Peter D Matthews

John was woken one morning with a commotion of diggers yelling below. He went down asking, 'whatever is the matter'.

Little did anyone know that police reinforcements had arrived during the night, with an extra 35 mounted police and 17 foot police.

The digger angrily garbled, 'In the thick of night, the blue-pissants pounced on the camp while we were all sound asleep. They arrested McIntyre, Fletcher and Yorkie (real name Henry Westoby). They dragged 'em off in chains and charged 'em with riot and burning the Eureka Hotel.'

'Interesting' John thought.

Three of his digger mates were accused of being the ringleaders of a so-called riot when the riot act had not been read. Let alone they were not responsible for the destruction of the hotel.

'How could this be?' John thought.

John knew who burnt down the Eureka Hotel. It certainly was not McIntyre, nor Fletcher or even Yorkie. It was Henry Goodenough! John had seen him with his own eyes.

But John kept quiet, holding his tongue, just as Dr Carr advised. Otherwise he would be next. John had seen firsthand the corruption within the government camp. Not wanting to attract any attention, he quietly went back to Dalton's Flat to work on the goldfields, leaving Margaret at the hotel.

Dalton's Gold
By Peter D Matthews

Attack Against the Catholic Church

In reward for the so-called riot, you guessed it, Rede came out for another licence hunt, but this time with more ferocity.

Johannes McGregorius was a meek Armenian disabled man who was the servant of Father Patrick Smyth of St Alipius Catholic Church. He was visiting a digger laid up sick in his tent on top of Bakers Hill.

At the time John was heading down Bakers Hill towards Dalton's Flat and saw the entire event.

A trooper named James Lord rode up to the door of the tent McGregorious was visiting and yelling out, 'Get out here you damned wretches. Got your licences?'

Johannes in broken English answered, 'I am servant to priest, Father Smyth. I here attending sick.'

The angry trooper screamed, 'Damn you and the priest' as he dismounted his horse.

He grabbed Johannes by the scruff of the neck. Johannes protested that he was disabled, and unable to walk over the diggings. The trooper knocked him to the ground, beating the disabled servant severely with a clenched fist.

Diggers all around yelled in protest, 'Shame on you beating a disabled man. You're a disgrace.'

Assistant Commissioner Johnson rode up telling off the crowd of diggers, saying, 'Do not interfere with him doing his duty, or I'll have you all locked up'.

John heard this and ran to get Father Smyth who was nearby. Father Smyth ran back with John and handed Johnson a five pound note, pleading 'Please take this as bail. I will make sure he is in attendance tomorrow and the police camp. Let me attend his wounds.'

To everyone's disgust, on attendance to the police camp the next morning, Johannes McGregorius was charged with being on the goldfields without a licence.

Appearing in the courtroom, Johannes tried to make a defence, only to be cut short and fined five pound.

John Dalton and Patrick Smyth talked to Assistant Commissioner Johnson on Johannes' behalf just outside the court. At that moment Johnson steamed into the courtroom as the matter was concluding.

John expected Johnson to stop the proceedings and drop the charges. Instead he yelled, 'McGregory (not able to pronounce his real name) is not charged with being without a licence but with assaulting the trooper', while looking back at John with a smile.

The trooper who was waiting outside, was called into the courtroom and testified how he was assaulted while carrying out his duty in a licence hunt.

John stood there gob smacked that the trooper would lie straight faced to the court. John's fury burnt inside him until he couldn't hold it in anymore.

'Excuse me, your worship. I saw the whole matter. May I take the stand to testify?' jumps in John Dalton.

'Very well. State you name, occupation, and what you saw?' the magistrate questioned.

'My name is John Thomas Dalton. I am a free settler to this country, not a convict like many of these Vandemonian's. I am a qualified boot maker, and a miner. I saw the trooper James Lord ride up demanding they come out of the tent, calling them "damned wretches". This man (pointing to Johannes) told the trooper that he was the servant of the priest and he was there attending the sick. He told the trooper that he was disabled and Lord struck McGregorius to the ground and beat him to senselessness. Upon seeing this I ran to get Father Smyth who was nearby. At no time did I see the servant strike the trooper. The trooper savagely and disgracefully beat this disabled man without reason, cursing the servant and the priest.'

Upon finishing his testimony the magistrates nodded his head allowing John to remove himself from the witness box.

Without hesitation the magistrate concluded the matter. In a rather disinterested but solemn tone he grunted, 'Guilty. Fined 5 pounds. Take him away.'

A meeting was held at the Catholic Chapel on Bakers Hill on Sunday 22th October 1854 to protest over the treatment of the servants of the Catholic Church. Their grievances were not just by the trooper James Lord but Commissioner Johnson for protecting the trooper, and the Ballarat Bench for fining Johannes five pound.

Lord was a well known English Protestant from Lancashire who hated Catholics, particularly Irish Catholics. This brought great resentment as a great majority of the population on the diggings were Catholic, and many of them of Irish origin.

The diggers were a respectable group of God fearing men and women. They had been beaten and robbed by the police, military, and even government officials. They were treated with contempt and called 'vagabonds' by the Victorian Government. Although really it was the government's lack of services and infrastructure that forced many of them to live in squaller.

That could be tolerated but to insult their religion, and the priest himself, was the straw that broke the camel's back. This in the eyes of the Ballarat Catholic congregation was completely intolerable.

John was asked by Father Patrick Smyth to testify before the crowd of almost 4,000 diggers as he did in the courtroom.

It was Sunday 22nd October 1854 after the Sunday service. Timothy Hayes, a devout Catholic, who was originally from Kilkenny, chaired the meeting. Hayes was a good mate and business partner on Eureka with Peter Lalor.

John spoke to the diggers giving an exact account of what happened to Johannes McGregorius. The crowd of angry diggers roared at the persecution by the Victorian government against the a servant of the

Church. Father Smyth arose and spoke to the crowd gathered outside the church, calling for peace.

Hayes called for a collection to defend the diggers arrested in connection with the Eureka Hotel. He asserted that the government were responsible in one way or another for provoking the meeting, and of course for the general mismanagement of the goldfields. All agreed with shouting from the crowd.

Hands were raised to vote and it was unanimously decided to establish a society for diggers rights. John put up both of his hands to show his sincerity. Hayes turned to John who was standing near the front, saying, 'Dalton and I are both head and shoulders above most of you, therefore we're allowed two votes', having a chuckle with the crowd.

They voted again to send a letter to Governor Hotham on behalf of the Ballarat Catholics. The vote was unanimous with of course an extra vote each from Dalton and Hayes.

They diggers agreed to 'demand' an inquiry into the conduct of the officers concerned. It was customary to petition and pray for God's intervention, but not on this occasion. The diggers were up to their eye teeth, and it was time to make demands.

They voted to demand reform of the treatment of diggers, and demand their civil rights be recognized as citizens, allowing them to vote.

The gathering caught the attention of the Commissioner with such a large crowd. This show of force was recognized by Rede as disrespectful, and licence hunts were increased to almost every other day but more brutal than ever.

John likened it to poking a dog with a stick in a corner. It might put up with being hit every so often and just cower. But to be beaten and oppressed every single day, sooner or later the dog will no doubt come out of the corner snarling and growling refusing to take it anymore.

Ballarat Reform League

Seven more diggers were arrested in connection with the Eureka Hotel fire, and on Wednesday 1st November 1854 some 3,000 diggers met at Bakery Hill.

The meeting of diggers were addressed by Thomas Kennedy, Henry Holyoake, George Black and Henry Ross. John at the time could not make it to the meeting because he was making preparations for the wedding on 20th November which was less than three weeks away.

Kennedy was a Scotsman and mate of James Scobie. Holyoake was an English political activist. Black was also from England but he generally kept to himself. Henry Ross was a fellow Canadian and good mate of John's from Ontario.

Henry came from a military family. He was always talking of his grandfather's Scottish background as Quartermaster in the Scottish Light Infantry, who stayed in Canada after the war. Henry's father was also in the Toronto Militia. He was taken prisoner by US troops. Therefore, Henry had come from a family that was accustomed to military conflict.

What an assorted bunch of diggers they were. All of whom were free colonial settlers from all over the world. Yet willing to stand for each other as mates, side-by-side, for their civil rights.

It was not until Saturday 11th November 1854 that the Ballarat Reform League was officially birthed where a crowd of over 10,000 diggers gathered at Bakery Hill.

John Basson Humffray who was a lawyer, come gold digger, chaired the meeting. He seemed to be more interested in the rights of the miners more than the exorbitant licence fees.

Humffray was a typical lawyer - outspoken, convincing, opinionated, but far too forthright in his demands. He had dark curly hair, always neat and perfectly placed with a curly short beard to match. His complexion pale, sunken eyes and large crooked nose which seemed in keeping with his personality. Like many lawyers, they appear to be your friend, that is until you are no longer needed or you run out of money. Hence Humffray was friend to John Dalton while it suited him - especially when he needed a new pair of boots!

In his chairing of the meeting, Humffray laid down some of the basic rights that diggers should be given as colonial settlers. These rights were no different to immigrating pastoralists already received. Humffray said:

> That, as all men are born free and equal, this meeting demands the right to a voice in the framing of the laws which they are called on to obey... we must not omit to mention a strong conviction in the minds of diggers, that they will never have justice until they are fairly and fully represented in the Legislative Council ... and we would respectfully suggest, for the serious consideration of His Excellency, the justice of at once giving full and fair representation to the people... While England is under the necessity of advancing towards the development of her constitution by gradual concessions, we, who have nothing to do with privileged classes, and vested political rights, had the choice of at once beginning a new career.[2]

Humffray suggested it was time to make a stand, not in violence, but in demanding reform from Governor Hotham and the Legislative Council.

The changes they demanded were:
A full and fair representation on the Legislative Council (Victorian Parliament), representing diggers;
Manhood suffrage - the right to vote, as diggers were regarded as lower class vagabonds, and were not entitled to vote.

One man, one vote, was the cry of the day;
No property qualification for members of the Legislative Council. The Legislative Council Parliament was exclusive to the independently wealthy, whereas the diggers believed any of them should be allowed to be elected from the working class;
Wages should be paid to persons who sit on the Legislative Council;
Short term of Parliament;
Abolition of diggers and storekeepers licences;
Reform of the administration of the goldfields, by immediately disbanding the commissioners, and the cruel method of collecting the taxes by force.

    Many of John's mates came to Australia as free settlers for a new start. They did not want to see replicated similar tyrannical governments they had come from. They wanted a say as stakeholders in the future of their newly settled country. If they were going to move half way around the world, and put their heart and soul into the country, they wanted some say in its future.
    Meanwhile extra troops were being brought in to Ballarat which concerned John. He had no desire to die for the cause, as some suggested, but John merely

wanted reform. He had a beautiful fiancé that he was about to marry. With his heart firmly fixed upon his bride, he decided it best to remain quiet and reserved at the meeting.

The meeting was followed by another meeting on 18th November 1854 where John Humffray, Thomas Kennedy and George Black were elected as delegates to present the diggers demands direct to the Governor Hotham himself in Melbourne. This was just in case the diggers message wasn't getting through to him via Rede.

He left the meeting as soon as it was concluded as he was rather preoccupied with the upcoming wedding which by this time was only two days away.

John didn't like their chances after his experience with Hotham. Hotham had used the Gold Commissioner and corrupt Police to cheat him out of his gold.

The Long Awaited Wedding

The long awaited wedding day had come. Preparations were complete. Monday the 20th November 1854 finally had arrived.

Margaret rose early in the morning at the Bath Hotel. She had breakfast with Alice, her best friend and bridesmaid.

Dr Carr was not invited to the wedding. He knew nothing of the wedding. Margaret had changed her name to Margaret 'Carry' to disassociate herself from her uncle.

Upon the request of Margaret, Thomas Bath had prepared a special early 'high tea' for Margaret's breakfast. Margaret had invited Alice to join her, along with Mrs Carr, without the knowledge her husband of course.

The fine white linen tablecloth with the best silverware in the colony, and the most decadent gold leafed fine bone china, was a special gesture provided by Thomas Bath. This sort of opulence was normally only provided to royalty.

John woke up with a completely different view to that of his bride. He had booked a room for the night at the George Inn which was only just a few doors down from the Bath Hotel. John had planned to stay there for the night.

Instead John woke up lying face down in the dirt. He was filthy and seemed to be covered in what appeared to be his own vomit. All he could muster was an 'Oohhh'.

As he rolled over he realized he had slept the night face down outside Carboni's tent. He looked up and there was Carboni cooking breakfast over the fire with Tobias McGrath.

McGrath said, 'You're finally awake. We've got breakfast just about ready for you. Looks like you had a bit too much of the good stuff last night.'

John somehow ended up back at the camp instead of the George Inn, but poor John couldn't remember a thing. The last thing he remembered was drinking at the bar with a group of his mates.

With a pounding hangover, McGrath dragged John up to start the day with a little whiskey before breakfast. John was not hungry at all, but McGrath forced him to eat the lamb chops he and Carboni had prepared, before they headed back to the George Inn for a shower.

After all it was Tobias McGrath who promised Margaret to make sure he was at the wedding on time. McGrath was the best man at the wedding. John had asked Carboni to be the best man but Carboni cared little for the sanctity of marriage or so he said. John thought it was more likely that he just hadn't found the right one yet.

The time had come for the bride to depart the Bath Hotel. John had organised a magnificent horse drawn carriage even though it was not far to St Alipius Catholic Church.

What a sight for all to see as she was ushered into the carriage!

Her wedding dress consisted of a white four flounced cartridge pleated white skirt and a fan front white bodice with capped close fitting long sleeves. It was graced with a veil attached to a coronet of pink flowers. She wore short white kid gloves with a handkerchief embroidered with her initials 'MC'. Her shoes were special handmade white shoes, personally hand decorated by John with pink ribbons at the instep.

Margaret arrived at St Alipius Church. Carboni breathlessly whispered, 'Margaret guarda gorgeous. Molto bello.'

'What does that mean?' John asked, thinking he had a fair idea.

'Margaret is gorgeous. Everything is beautiful' Carboni gasps.

McGrath cheekily acknowledged, 'She does scrub up pretty well'.

John just stood there dumb-founded without a word, almost awestruck by her beauty. He was in his best suit, but compared to Margaret, he felt underdressed.

As she walked down the aisle between the old wooden pews, the music started playing Wagner's Bridal Chorus for the first time on the new organ. It was just built by George Fincham, a Ballarat parishioner and organ maker, just before he left the goldfields for Melbourne.

Father Smyth conducted a fairly short but solemn service simply exchanging vows and signing the register. When it came time to kiss the bride, John pulled Margaret right in close. She leaned her head back as John lifted her veil. Although he was almost six inches taller, Margaret lifted herself almost eye to eye, while John dipped his knees to assist.

John's lips had been ready for that moment from the very time he laid his eyes on her aboard the Araminta. The long awaited kiss was more than any kiss he had given before. His lips overpowered her, and he refused to let go. He had waited so long to stand together with Margaret as his wife.

Their thirty second embrace seemed to last forever. In the end Father Smyth had to step in to separate them, mumbling, 'Come on. There's time for that later.'

    The women in the congregation blushed and had a little chuckle. The men however were applauding and cheering John on. Finally the long awaited day had come and John married his sweetheart, Margaret. This was the best day of his life.

    Arm in arm, John and Margaret headed off to their reception at the Bath Hotel, to enjoy each other's company and celebrate with their mates.

    John had a present sitting at the Bath Hotel for his best mates. Peter Lalor, Raffaello Carboni and Tobias McGrath had no idea what John had prepared.

    Quality clothing and handmade boots were beyond most Victorian settlers. Miners even more so, as their boots would disintegrate in no time on the diggings. Many of them had to acquire John's services in the regular upkeep of their boots.

    Margaret had helped John craft custom-made black watertight boots without any of his mates knowing. She had secured the best black calfskin from Geelong, and John handcrafted each pair at night before the wedding.

    They were made from the very best extremely supple black calfskin leather. The boots were trimmed to fit closely around the leg at mid-calf height with low cut heels about an inch. Having worked on their boots many times before he knew their fitting size off the top of his head.

Dalton's Gold
By Peter D Matthews

These custom boots were the first ever made Victorian boots for the goldfields to be watertight during the day, and if polished up they were suitable for evening wear. They were called 'Dalton's Watertight Gentry Boots' modelled on the watertight calfskin boots of the Duke of Wellington but with John's own local Victorian twist.

Carboni excitedly put on his new black watertight gentry boots and tromped around the camp as proud as punch. In fact Carboni secured John twenty orders for custom-made watertight gentry boots within a week. Actually Carboni loved them so much that John never saw Carboni take them off!

The diggers sat back at ease at the reception not having a care in the world. They were completely unaware that many of their mates celebrating with them would lay dead or arrested for high treason in the coming days.

7
THE SOUTHERN CROSS SHINES

There was commotion in the streets below on Saturday 25th November 1854, just a few days after the wedding. John and Margaret were still honeymooning at the Bath Hotel when all of a sudden there was a knock at the door.

'Just a moment' John yelled, as he slipped on some trousers to go downstairs.

It was Carboni and McGrath standing there with a newspaper in their hands. John shut the door behind him allowing Margaret to sleep in. After all, it was still their honeymoon.

'Sorry to wake you but you need to see this' Carboni said, as he passed John a newspaper.

John read the Ballarat Times:

Trial of Mr & Mrs Bentley, Hanse and Farrel, for the murder of James Scobie, in the Supreme Court of Melbourne. Guilty of Manslaughter. Mrs Bentley scot-free. His Honour considered their conduct was wanton and reckless. He should mark his sense of outrage of which they have been found guilty by passing on each of them a sentence of 3 years imprisonment with hard labour on the roads.[3]

John was sick in the stomach by the time he finishes reading the article. Then McGrath grumbled, 'You haven't seen the worst of it yet. Read this one.'

Trial of Fletcher, McIntyre and Westoby, for burning the Eureka Hotel, in the Supreme Court, Melbourne. Guilty, with a recommendation to mercy!

The Foreman of the Jury appended the following rider to the verdict: 'The Jury feel, in giving their verdict against the prisoners at the bar, that in all probability, they (the jury) should never have had that painful duty to perform, if those entrusted with the government officers of Ballarat had done theirs properly.'

His Honour said: 'The sentence of the Court is, that you, McIntyre be confined in Her Majesties gaol at Melbourne for 3 months, but I shall not subject you to labour. You, Fletcher, to four months; and you Westoby, to six months confinement. The Executive was sufficiently strong to punish those who outrage the law!'[4]

John stood there with tears welling up in his eyes wondering whatever to do. He knew that it was not James Scobie that was buried, but knew if he spoke up that he would no doubt be framed for something, and taken off in shackles too. John never expected that Bentley would be gaoled. There was no evidence that he killed anyone. A lady and her son heard a few voices of a number of people but couldn't confirm who, then she heard a dull thud as if someone or something was hit. Bentley's merely advised that two men approached the hotel after it was closed and they told them to move on - nothing more. Who knows whether Scobie and Martin were ever there?

The Bentley's and other witnesses at the hotel confirmed that the Bentley's never even left the hotel. What was worse was that John had seen Scobie after the burning of the hotel. How could Bentley be convicted for a murder that he did not commit? John knew James Bentley was innocent but could not say a word.

What was even more despicable was that three of his mates had been gaoled for riot and the burning down of the Eureka Hotel, when he saw Henry Goodenough throw the burning torch into the rear of the Hotel. Afterward John saw Goodenough drinking with troopers, so something was seriously amiss, which pointed towards a government plot.

He thought, 'If I let on and it gets out that I said it, for sure I will meet an early grave. I've got no choice but button my lip if I want to live. Instead I will take this secret to my grave.'

'Dalton are you all right?' McGrath said, as he grabbed John's arm.

John was in a world of his own, deliberating his own predicament. Composing his thoughts, John agreed, 'That's terrible news. We all know it was not any of these diggers that burnt down the Eureka Hotel.'

Carboni announced, 'There is a monster meeting on Bakery Hill on Wednesday 29th November, so you better get your affairs in order or get of here with Margaret.'

John answered, 'You know how you told Thomas Bath that I was from Smythesdale? I have been thinking of moving out there. I'd like to set up a boot maker's shop, raise a family, and settle down a bit. There's been reports of quite a bit of alluvial gold found along Woady Yalloak Creek. I'll take Margaret out to Smythesdale for a couple of days to see if she likes the place, but I'll be back on Wednesday for the meeting.'

John and Margaret headed off on horseback to Smythesdale. As they rode through the green rolling hills overlooking Woady Yalloak Creek, Margaret was pleasantly surprised. There were only a few permanent buildings in those days. The newly built Court House Hotel was one of them. The weatherboard hotel was just the spot for a few nights while they adventured the region.

The following day they explored the diggings along Woady Yalloak Creek, and John was excited about the possibilities. It was a difficult choice to move though, as he would be further away from his mates.

John noticed a vacant plot of land near the hotel along Brooke Street and asked the hotel owner about it. Keen to have a boot maker in the region, he welcomed John and Margaret Dalton with open arms.

Dalton's Gold
By Peter D Matthews

John and Margaret stayed a few days. They were taken by the beauty of Smythesdale, and deciding it was where they wanted to settle down and raise a family.

Monster Meeting

On Wednesday 29th November 1854 they heading back to Ballarat and arrived just in time for the meeting. John rode past the site of the meeting on Bakery Hill. It seemed rather formal with a stage erected with diggers already starting to gather. At the edge of the stage was an impressive flagpole about 80 feet high, and on that flagpole was a flag being raised by Henry Ross. This was the flag of the Southern Cross.

The Southern Cross flag was Australia's first patriotic symbol. It was erected for the first time in Ballarat on 29th November 1854. Henry Ross who was a staunch Catholic, was the one who designed the rendition in his tent one night. He presented the design a couple of weeks earlier to Father Smyth along with Timothy Hayes and John Dalton, who were both deacons at St Alipius Catholic Church.

Ecclesiastical flags with a white cross were flown by many a church in those days to denote the service was about to begin. One was flown every service at St Alipius Catholic Church. John Dalton or Timothy Hayes were the two deacons entrusted with raising the flag for Father Smyth before the start of every service. The only difference with this flag was the addition of the five stars of the Southern Cross, and its gigantic size of course.

Anastasia Hayes, wife of Timothy Hayes, along with fellow parishioners of St Alipius Catholic congregation, created the flag from Henry Ross's design. The two ladies that assisted were Anastasia Withers and Anne Duke.

It was large blue silk flag about 14 feet wide by 8 feet high bearing nothing but the five white stars of Southern Cross constellation, linked with a vertical and horizontal cross, denoting the cross of Christ being central to their way of life.

The three ladies painstakingly overlaid the white silk stripes from their very own petticoats which made the flag glisten silver in the light.

John Dalton later recounted, 'The Southern Cross was our date with destiny. We were called to stand and were joined by our faith in God's promise to release us from tyranny.'

The Southern Cross was believed to be a sign from in the sky of God's promise of blessing and hope over Australia to these early settlers. These God fearing diggers believed the Southern Cross being flown so high in sky towards heaven would influence God to intervene, and change the mind of Hotham.

John dropped Margaret off at the Hotel, while he headed back to the meeting. John attended the meeting as he was interested to hear the report from the delegates who met with Hotham.

On the platform was Timothy Hayes who chaired the meeting with Humffray, Kennedy, Vern, Father Smyth, Father Downing and Dr Goold, the Melbourne

Catholic Bishop. Dr Goold stood there in all his regalia beside his Catholic priests. He had come at the request of Father Smyth to promote peace. This drew a group of reporters who also stood on the platform.

The delegates each were given the opportunity to speak to the crowd of about 15,000 diggers. Humffray said, 'I was received by Sir Charles. He understands our grievances and has agreed to appoint a Commission of Inquiry, and he is with us and will act accordingly.'

Humffray motioned, 'That the league protests against the common practice of police and military marching into a peaceable district with fixed bayonets, firing on the people, under any circumstances, without the previous reading of the Riot Act, and that if Government officials continue to act thus unconstitutionally, we cannot be responsible for similar or worse deeds from the people.'

The motion was seconded by Thomas Kennedy who was one of the other delegates sent to Hotham. Other diggers seemed to be arguing amongst themselves on the platform.

Up stands the towering Peter Lalor as it was clear that there was a split amongst the delegates. He proposed a resolution, 'That a meeting of the members of the Reform League be called at the Adelphi Theatre next Sunday at 2 pm to elect a central committee and that each fifty members of the League have power to elect one member for the central committee.'

By this time John Dalton was already a member and put his hand up to second the motion but was beaten by Hugh Brady who was another digger from Ireland, who worked down Magpie Gully.

Frederick Vern proposed a resolution, 'To burn our licences and pledge that in the event of any party being arrested for having no licenses, the united people will, under all circumstances, defend and protect them.'

The motion was seconded by Edward Quinn who a digger from Cavan in Ireland, who worked on Eureka close to where Lalor had previously worked. Father Downing appealed to the crowd to bring peace, and objected to the burning of licences. John didn't raise his hand in favour of burning the licences, as frankly he knew the outcome of not having a licence only too well.

Vern professed to be German but John coming from Canada knew Vern's accent was either from South America, Mexico or Peru. He was a trouble maker, and loved nothing more than a good old barney. He turned up on Dalton's Flat soon after John found the Lady Hotham nugget but all he did was argue and pick fights amongst the diggers.

George Black who was one of the delegates also proposed a resolution, 'That as the diggers have determined to pay no more licenses, it was not practical for the Gold Commissioner to resolve claim disputes, therefore the party appoint one man, the other party appoint one man, and together they appoint a third and the three decide the matter.'

The motion was seconded by Whately whom John had never met.

Patrick Murnane, a friend of Peter Lalor from Tipperary, proposed a motion, 'That this league will not be bound to protect any man after the 15th December who shall not be a member of the League by that day.'

The motion was seconded by Henry Ross.

In closing the tickets of membership were issued, and guns were fired into the air with excitement. Licences were burned in the streets in protest before the government camp.

Meanwhile the blue-pissants and red-toads were sneakily waiting in the gully beneath the camp, hoping for an outbreak of violence, but fortunately that never occurred.

John and his mates dispersed. John went back to Margaret at the Hotel, and his mates returned to their camp. After all it was back to work on the goldfields the next morning.

Final Licence Hunt

The general consensus was that the diggers were safe to go back to work. Nobody expected another licence hunt after Hotham had heard about the real feelings of the diggers.

It was mid morning on Dalton's Flat and John was working away on a new hole with three of his mates. The others didn't turn up for work.

All of sudden a digger came running through Dalton's Flat yelling, 'Licence hunt! Lalor is calling for all of us to fall-in on Bakery Hill.'

John dropped his pick, exchanging it for his new colt baby dragoon pistol, and headed off to the aid of Peter Lalor. He had bought the small inconspicuous .31 calibre single action revolver for his own protection after staring down the barrel of Goodenough's long and intimidating .44 calibre revolver.

The goldfields were a flurry of activity as all grabbed whatever they had to protect themselves, and rushed to Bakery Hill. Each man came with whatever he had: firearms, knives, swords, but if nothing else, the simple pick and shovel would do.

Upon arriving the blue-pissants were raiding the gravel pits. To object, the diggers pelted stones at the blue-pissants, and they had no choice but withdraw.

There was close to a thousand diggers assembled on the road with every manner of weapon to protect themselves. The blue-pissants stood back and called for Rede to come.

In typical Rede pomposity he came on horseback and just sat on his horse, refusing to alight. It seemed as if he delighted in sitting high above the diggers, like he was the king and they were his loyal subjects.

Lalor went forward and forthrightly boomed, 'We free colonial settlers will no longer be hunted like dogs. We will not produce licences. Send your pissants away.'

Rede argued with Lalor with Carboni at his side. Rede insisted, 'So long as the law is in force, I will maintain it. The intention of His Excellency the Lieutenant Governor Hotham was to abolish the license-fee if advised to do so by the commission. But until then, I will maintain the law.'

At that Carboni turned and walked away. He seemed satisfied that Rede's communication was enough. He merely accepted without any rebuttal that the diggers would be subject to licence hunts until the commission abolish the licence fee.

John grabbed Caroni by the arm, complaining, 'You don't honestly believe this gold laced swine that stands before us squealing like a lost piglet crying out for its mother? He has proven himself to be corrupt. We can't believe a word that comes out from his mouth.'

Carboni looked at John holding his arm indignantly, and looked up at John, openly stating, 'I am an Italian revolutionary. I do not believe in violent conflict, but peaceable unity. There is no need to clash as it only causes bloodshed.'

Meanwhile the stones just kept getting thrown at the blue-pissants. Rede himself was now the target. One un-named digger from behind John threw a rock which hit Rede in the head.

'That's it' Rede screamed as he called for reinforcements. The riot act was read and the line was drawn in the sand that the diggers dare not cross.

Many of the diggers followed Carboni and backed off from the conflict. At the point of rifle and bayonet some of the diggers showed their licences to Assistant Commissioner Johnston. Others shot their rifles and pistols into the air to show their disgust. One particular digger had his hand shot by a trooper after discharging his rifle.

As the government seized control, eight diggers without licences were carted off. The remainder of the diggers dispersed in fear of being slaughtered. Instead they decided to ready themselves just in case Rede continued his indiscriminate brutality in the slaughter of free citizens.

John followed Peter Lalor but was so surprised by Carboni's comments. John had spent considerable time with him and valued him as a friend. He had believed his revolutionary talk. John was astounded that when it came down to it, Carboni had no guts or fortitude - it was all just talk.

John knew Carboni was rather shrewd but did not expect him to back away from a fight. He had always promoted the fact of talking first to resolve the matter but asserted that if talks disintegrated, force may be the only option. Clearly Carboni was a coward in John's eyes, and they never really saw eye-to-eye again.

Bakery Hill was exposed and not a good position, therefore Lalor assembled the diggers and marched to Eureka where another meeting was held. John stood by Lalor. Both Lalor and Dalton were concerned that even though Carboni was trying to unite the diggers, he was actually creating a rift between those wanting action, and those seeking a more philosophical resolution.

Dalton's Gold
By Peter D Matthews

Dawn of the ANZAC Spirit

Lalor and Dalton arrived on Eureka. There was hardly a cloud in the sky. Henry Ross was there as caretaker of the flag, and hoisted the majestic blue flag high into a heavens. Ross posted himself below the pole with his sword in his hand, daring anyone come too near. He was ready to cut anyone down in an instant.

As men gathered from all around to hear, Peter Lalor had no choice but take the lead. He climbed up on a stump to unite his mates, destroying any chance of a rift. With his left hand on the muzzle of his rifle, and the butt of the rifle on his left foot, he quietened the crowd and said:

> It is my duty to swear you in and to take with you the oath to be faithful to the Southern Cross. Hear me with attention. The man who after this solemn oath does not stand by our standard is a coward in heart. I order all persons who do not intend to take the oath to leave the meeting at once. Let all divisions under arms fall-in in their order round the flag-staff.

John had resolved in his own heart, that it was time to stand, so he stood with his revolver in his hand, beside his mate Peter Lalor, in readiness to be sworn in. Others quickly gathered around their chosen leader.

Dalton's Gold
By Peter D Matthews

About 500 men stood around the flag that venerable day.

Peter Lalor climbed off the stump and approached the flagpole. He had determined in his heart that he would make a stand with his mates to defend their rights, even unto death.

With a solemn look upon his face, Peter removed his hat and knelt before the flag. The captains of each division made a military style salute to him. Looking unto heaven with the flag raised high, he shouted:

We swear by the Southern Cross to stand truly by each other and fight to defend our rights and liberties.

Not a single man stood there without a hand raised. John Thomas Dalton with five hundred of his mates stood with their faces toward the heavens. Each and every one had decided to stand. Each one swore an oath to protect each other's rights and liberties.

This was the birth of the ANZAC spirit in Australia. Courageous or stupid you may question, but these five hundred diggers had seen too many of their mates chased like foxes by Vandemonian dogs, only to be shot in the back or bayoneted to death. It was time to stand - live or die - they could take no more.

No longer were they separated by nationality or stature. Natural born Australians stood side-by-side with immigrants and pardoned ex-convicts. They stood there united as free men under the flag of the Southern Cross. There were doctors, lawyers, farmers, miners and tradespeople alike. They all stood shoulder-to-shoulder so to speak, in defence of each other. No longer were they going to be treated with contempt or hunted like dogs in the name of tax collection. It was time to a stand side-by-side, mate alongside mate, to defend each other to the bitter end.

All pitched in gathering slabs of timber and overturning carts to set up a barrier around the camp on Eureka. They used whatever they could find - after all something was better than nothing at all. No more were they going to be attacked and plundered by surprise. Next time they would be ready.

Meanwhile a drunken digger staggered out of the crowd, and started burning down other diggers tents. He was laughing and jeering, no different to the stinking blue-pissant Vandemonians. John could not see his face but could hear his voice and knew who it was.

Carboni raced towards him with a sword so John followed with his revolver drawn just in case there was trouble. Upon turning the digger around, Carboni found it was Henry Goodenough.

John grabbed Goodenough with one arm and in the other was his revolver pointed directly at Goodenough. He tried talking to him in his drunken stupor. Goodenough blurted out, 'You're all going to die, you dirty rotten vagabonds'.

Carboni was normally self controlled, but this time he did not stop to hear the answer. He booted Goodenough so hard in the groin that Goodenough dropped to the ground.

Dalton's Gold
By Peter D Matthews

John picking him up shouting, 'On your way and sober up'. John could not shoot him even though he really thought about it. This is something the blue-pissants would do and John could not stoop to their level.

As Goodenough staggered off into the distance, the diggers started drilling military style under the leadership of Frederick Vern. Little did Dalton or Carboni realize that Goodenough staggered back to the government camp. Although a deceitful lie, as retribution, Goodenough told Rede that the diggers were planning an attack on the government camp.

The sadistic treacherous gold laced Rede had a plan in mind and the diggers had no idea.

Over the following couple of days the diggers worked on the 'ring' around the camp, or stockade as the government called it. But it was never designed to be a fortified stockade. Really it was 'a ring' or 'circle' around the camp as an enclosure to allow the diggers to drill and prepare themselves.

John Dalton described, 'The ring was erected not as a military structure, but to keep government spies out, and allow us the time to prepare so that we may defend ourselves if the government did attack us as we were told. It was nothing more than a fence, as an early protection mechanism for our own safety.'

Dr Carr sent message to John to come to the hospital. John headed off thinking one of his mates may be injured. Arriving at the hospital, Dr Carr said to John:

You and I may not see eye-to-eye but I know you are a friend of Peter Lalor who seems to be the one in charge of the diggers. Rede is planning to attack your stockade. I heard him saying to senior officers 'My orders are to quell the miners at any cost. We need to crush this movement and slaughter all of these damned diggers'. Please, you must talk to Lalor!

'Why should I listen to you. You have lied to me. You have betrayed Margaret and I. She is now my wife, therefore you have betrayed your own family. Why should I believe you now' John indignantly scoffed.

Dr Carr begged, 'Very simply Dalton, I promised my brother William Carr that I would protect Margaret. If you won't listen to me, then at least send her back to me for a few days so that I may keep her safe here. Please allow me to keep that promise to your father-in-law, whom you have never met.'

'Fine' said John, 'But if anything happens to her, your assistant here will be doing an autopsy on your body by day's end.'

John went back to the Hotel and asked Margaret to stay with her Uncle for a few days for her own protection. John promised to visit her every day so that she would know that he was safe.

John set off for the stockade on Eureka to talk to his mate Lalor about what Dr Carr had just revealed.

Vern, Lalor, and Carboni were there. Lalor listened to what John had to say about Dr Carr but was cautious as they all knew Dr Carr was a government spy.

Carboni refused to listen to what Dr Carr had said. Instead he sniggered, 'Rede is using him to convince us to lay down our arms so that they can just come in and slaughter us like beasts'.

John suggested, 'But if he is right we will be slaughtered. Why not negotiate with Rede, in laying down our arms so that we can all live to fight another day?'

Vern barked, 'Don't listen to him. This is a trap from Rede. If we lay down our arms that will be the end of us. We must defend.'

Even though John had spoke with Lalor, Carboni and Vern, they didn't seem to take him seriously. They continued building the stockade, so all John could do, was pitch in. He helped gather whatever he could to help his mates.

But Peter pondered this thought the rest of the afternoon. 'What if Dr Carr is right? Maybe we could negotiate with Rede now that he knows our demands' Lalor blurted all of a sudden.

John agreed, 'We can only try'.

Last Ditched Effort for Peace

Lalor called a meeting on dusk with all of the elected Captains. After the meeting Peter told John, 'We have decided to send one last deputation to Rede based upon Dr Carr's advice. We have agreed to lay down our arms and return to work, on two conditions. One, the diggers arrested are released; and two, there are no more licence hunts.'

'Thanks Peter. We have given it our best and now all we can do is hope and pray that Rede agrees' John sighed deeply as he hoped for the best.

Raffaello Carboni, George Black and Father Patrick Smyth were the delegates sent to Rede, that dark and ominous evening. The skies were clear and the moon was bright, but nothing as compared to the brilliance of the Southern Cross, that shone down as the diggers approached the government camp.

This was the diggers last ditched effort to stop the violence and bloodshed. Did the sky project a positive outcome? Would they come back with a positive resolution or would the government resort to innocent bloodshed?

The delegates were met with a strong arm of blue-pissants guarding the bridge into the government camp. The camp was overrun with red-toads who were clearly preparing for war but war upon who?

The answer may curdle your blood, and even send shivers down your spine, but the truth must come out. They were preparing to go to war against Australia's own hard working oppressed diggers!

John along with about eight hundred other diggers, lined the main road that led into the government camp, anxiously waiting for the delegates to return.

Dalton's Gold
By Peter D Matthews

Carboni thought with his elegant speech that he could win over Commissioner Rede, not realizing that Rede's intention was to provoke them to take up arms, which would enable Rede to lawfully wipe out the protesting diggers.

As they came out of the government camp, their faces said it all. Dissatisfaction mushrooming into fury would not adequately describe their long and weary faces.

As they arrived back at the stockade, George Black spoke first, saying, 'I plainly and straightforwardly told Mr Rede of our exasperation. I told him we will not put up with him shooting down our mates just because he has no licence on him. We will not be terrorized by brutal soldiery and I laid out our demands. Rede sat there indignantly in his gold laced cap and insulted us, believing we wanted a democratic revolution. In the end, he clenched his hands and covered Carboni's joined hands of prayer, as if to crush Carboni's hands. He said, "My dear fellow, the licence is a mere watchword of the day and they make a cat's paw of you. Understand me, gentlemen, I give no pledge."'

Every digger knew what that meant. This phrase came from an old 16th century fable of the clever monkey which persuaded the cat to use its paw to take roasted chestnuts out of burning coals, thereby the monkey strategically got the chestnuts, and the cat was burnt in the process.

For all Carboni's education, he did not catch on to what Rede was saying, even though most of the uneducated diggers did.

Rede was literally saying, 'I have taken advantage of you and you weren't even smart enough to catch on. I am not here to negotiate, but to enforce the law, and if that means strategically using you as pawns to destroy you, so be it. Yet you are so stupid that you do not even see it - you will burned like the cat.'

As part of Rede's strategy, the diggers took this response and phraseology as a sign of hard lined commissioner who was willing to do anything to crush them. The diggers had little choice. It was defend or die.

Word was sent to the diggers at Bendigo, Castlemaine, and Creswick. Digger reinforcements were expected from all of these areas to support the Ballarat diggers in a stand against a tyrannical government.

The next day came. It was Friday 1st December 1854, and not a single digger turned up for work on the goldfields of Ballarat. All the diggers assembled armed on Eureka ready to drill, after Rede's pigheaded refusal to stop the persecution and free the diggers wrongfully arrested.

Mid morning word came that red-toads were assembling in preparation for another licence hunt. Peter Lalor gave the command to take our positions around the stockade, and be alert ready to defend.

Had Commissioner Rede attacked at that time with 800 men at the ready in the stockade, they would have had their hands full to say the least. However this

Dalton's Gold
By Peter D Matthews

strategic move by Rede allowed him to see exactly what the diggers would do in the event that the government forces did attack. The government forces were outnumbered and didn't attack. Like cunning dogs, they sat back quietly monitoring, stalking their prey. They almost mesmerized the diggers, like a snake charmer luring them into his deceitful scheme of devastation.

Their only real lack was arms and ammunition. They had very little of both. John only had six balls and caps, plus a flask of powder that was almost empty. Lalor sent out for as much ammo as they could find, honestly of course. Those that could not afford to pay, borrowed from their mates. John couldn't manage to buy any more ammo in the whole camp as there were no supplies to buy. The poor diggers were practically unarmed.

Lalor asked who had blacksmith skills that could make pikes. Pikes had been used in wars dating back into the middle ages. Peter knew of them from the battle of Vinegar Hill between the English and Irish at Wexford in Ireland. The idea of the pikes were to stop the troopers and cavalry just running through and slaughtering the diggers on horseback, thereby giving them half a chance. They were long timber or steel poles with a steel spearhead.

Johann Hafele, a digger from Württemberg, Germany, was a man that surprised everyone. He had never mentioned it but was a craftsman blacksmith, and had fashioned pike spearheads prior to coming to Australia, for battles in Mexico.

His work was impeccable - far beyond anything John had ever seen. Carboni enjoyed running Johann down, so John had not paid much attention to him on the goldfields. Carboni could speak German, although not too well. Johann could speak fluent German, French and English. So John thought Carboni felt more than a little threatened by Johann. He was at the most 5 feet tall, quiet stout, with a long wiry beard. He was as strong as an ox but had a tongue like an asp.

Johann spent all day around the fire, hammering and pointing to forge spearheads for the pikes. He swore that, 'My pikes will fix those red-toads and blue-pissants especially.'

Johann's steel spearheads with a reinforced shaft were designed to fasten to long well seasoned timber poles, so that the diggers could thrust them into the horses, thereby destroying their cavalry.

Loggers were sought to go into the scrub to select the right timbers, and carpenters to taper the poles to suit the spearheads.

Preparations went on all day with men gathering and manufacturing arms, to protect themselves from the tyrannical government, who were set on persecuting and killing innocent diggers.

Creswick Diggers

Thomas Kennedy rode into town late afternoon on horseback with a huge crowd of about four hundred diggers from Creswick. The self professed instigator of the Ballarat Reform League had set off days before to call the diggers of Creswick to arms. 'The more the merrier' was Kennedy's cry.

In his haste and determination to secure help, Kennedy assured his Creswick mates that they only needed to bring themselves. The Creswick diggers were told that there was plenty of food, grog, arms and ammunition at Ballarat. Finding it hard going at Creswick they were only too happy to lend a hand.

The Ballarat diggers welcomed them with open arms but as they all arrived late in the afternoon and the Ballarat diggers had no idea they were coming, they didn't have enough food to look after them.

Many of the Creswick diggers upon arrival, finding Kennedy was only giving them lip service to gather more troops, headed back to Creswick. Those that decided to stay were rather irate at being misled. The Ballarat diggers however stepped in. Edward Thonen was the purveyor (grocer). He supplied whatever was needed. George Bostock, the owner of the Eureka Butchery, provided the meat. His shop was opposite where the Eureka Hotel once was. The local baker provided the bread, and Peter Lalor provided the grog. All the diggers put in together so that the Ballarat storekeepers were not out of pocket.

At the large campfire in the middle of the stockade, they sat around drinking and chatting about their exploits. This didn't impress John much, so he went to visit Margaret and didn't return until later that evening.

Unfortunately some of the Creswick diggers were bitterly disappointed, and went around the town creating a ruckus. Some unfortunately went around stealing from a few of the local businesses in Ballarat. The shopkeepers thought that Lalor was behind the thieving, but this was not the case. Peter Lalor paid for everything he bought for the Creswick diggers.

John stayed in Peter Lalor's timber skillion shanty that evening on Eureka. It had a false timber floor with a hole beneath it. John had helped Peter dig out under the floor after their gold was stolen by Rede. It was the perfect place to hide just in case Rede and his demons came unannounced.

Drilling

With the larger number of diggers, Vern decided to enlarge the stockade to make room enough for drilling.

There was quite a bit of disarray so Lalor called in the diggers. He set them into companies according to their arms with two officers to each company. They were called rangers, pikemen, riflemen, and so on.

John Dalton was responsible for protecting Peter Lalor at all costs. Any group without a leader are destined to failure, so John pledged his allegiance to protect his mate.

There were seven companies with about seven hundred men. John fell in under the command of Peter Lalor.

Carboni was a sight though. He led a group of non-English speaking diggers with swords, and those with nothing more than knives. He told tales of his Italian military training, although really his style emulated the English military drilling. He marched his men two abreast just like the English, with Carboni at the side with his sword raised. It looked more like an ostentatious ceremonial procession. Carboni didn't realize it, but he was laughing stock of the stockade.

Michael Hanrahan was the captain of the pikeman. He trained the pikemen to bring down the cavalry, in the hope that if the government did attack, at least the diggers would have some fighting chance.

John, as part of the rifle company, marched all morning under the command of Peter Lalor. He trained alongside the pikeman so they could prepare for a cavalry advance. Hanrahan shouted, 'pick up poles'. Then, 'shoulder poles'. Then, 'ground poles' before, 'stand at ease'.

Marching continued with 'quick march' followed by, 'right counter march', then 'right face'. Finally Hanrahan yelled, 'Fall in three deep'. In military style they repeatedly trained in readiness, just in case of an attack.

'Prepare to receive the Cavalry' Hanrahan shouted, then 'Charge Cavalry'. As the pikemen ran forward Hanrahan yelled, 'Poke your pike into the guts of the horse and draw it out from under their tail'.

As the pikemen stepped back, Lalor shouted, 'Rifleman at the ready'. The rifle brigade advanced, taking their positions. 'Take aim' Lalor yelled. Lalor didn't want to waste ammunition, so the rifles were not loaded, but were at least the diggers were trained in sequence to know what to do should the need arise. 'Fire' was the command that everyone was waiting for.

'At ease' finally came and John was famished from all the drilling, so he headed off to meet Margaret for dinner.

All of the local diggers headed off from the stockade as it seemed to everyone that the government forces were not going to carry out another licence hunt as they had been told.

After all it was Saturday evening and the government wouldn't attack on Sunday morning, being the Sabbath. Or would they?

Salvation or Deliberate Deception?

John heard a commotion about 4:00pm that Saturday afternoon so he headed back to the Eureka camp to see what was going on. Upon arriving back at the camp he noticed about two hundred heavily armed horsemen who looked and dressed like Americans that he had seen before in Canada. They carried revolvers and American style bowie knives, along with rifles tucked into a saddle sling. The American bowie knife, commonly used by butchers in Canada, stood out to John in particular.

The long 30cm long blade with a backed out rear edge made the knife double edged, and its streamlined tip made it super sharp. It was perfect for deep penetration when stabbing or slashing the neck, while the brass quillon protected the users hand. This was the very weapon of choice used by the rangers back home, who were known to be coldheartedly brutal.

    Outside the stockade were posted these Independent Californian Rangers who stopped anyone entering unless the digger knew the password. Realizing who John was talking to, he immediately dropped his Irish accent, speaking in his native Canadian brogue, but with an American twist. The early Canadian English language was subtly different to American English and John knew the differences. So he decided to pose as a Californian Ranger.

    He tipped the front of his hat and nodded his head just as the Rangers did. The ranger could clearly see he was dressed like and American and he had an American colt pistol. With an American swagger, John simply voiced, 'What's Up'. This was a well known American slang and the ranger thought he was one them, and had just returned from scouting the area. The ranger let John into the stockade without a password.

    Their leader, James McGill, was in talks with Lalor and Vern. John couldn't even get in to see Peter Lalor. He was forced to wait outside the tent for some time, before they came out.

    Apparently McGill was friends with Vern, and these were the so-called German Rifle Brigade that Vern had been bandying about who would come to their rescue.

Dalton's Gold
By Peter D Matthews

This solidified John's suspicions that Frederick Vern was not who he said he was. If his men were American, Canadian, Scandinavian and Mexican, no doubt John was right that Vern was in fact Mexican or Peruvian.

'Who was Vern really?' John thought. He wondered if he was there to help or hinder? Their arrival encouraged most of the diggers, but John didn't trust either Vern or McGill. He couldn't put his finger on it, but something was up.

Then John heard that McGill had trained at West Point, which was a well renowned American military academy. The plot thickened. But yet McGill had setup sentry points keeping lookout for blue-pissants and red-toads, while checking those leaving or entering the stockade. So he thought there must be some merit in having them there, otherwise Peter Lalor would not have allowed him to become second in command.

Word soon came by one of McGill's men that the whole of road to Melbourne was swarming with more military reinforcements from Hotham. Word also came from the government camp that Hotham had ordered Rede, 'To crush the uprising of diggers using military force if necessary to suppress danger of insurrection'.

John tried again to talk to Peter Lalor but they remained huddled away and he was refused access. With a flurry of activity, most of the Independent Californian Rangers rode off towards Melbourne under the command of James McGill, to intercept the incoming red-toads. They took with them the majority of the ammo, as they insisted they required the ammo to take down the military.

Word came about 1:00am that some arms and ammo were secretly housed at Bakery Hill. So Henry Ross, who was Captain of the rifle division, rode off the with some of the Independent Californian Rangers through the bush, to replenish their supplies.

Dalton, Carboni, Lalor, Thonen and a number of their mates waited patiently around the fire for their return. By this time, it was almost 3:00am on Sunday morning 3rd December 1854, and there were only about one hundred and twenty diggers left in the stockade. With them was but a handful of rifles, pistols, knives and about twenty or so pikes.

Having stayed awake all night they were completely exhausted. While nervously waiting for McGill & Ross' return, the diggers pondered their fate. Peter Lalor was sitting around the fire on an old log, just outside his timber shanty. He confessed before all of his mates present, 'My friends, whatever happens in the next few days, whether we live or die, at least we have stood united. I am proud to have serve with you and call you my mates.'

'Here, here. Three cheers for Lalor' John shouted. All cheered as they raised their glasses of fine Irish Whiskey around the fire together.

Little did they know that for many of them, this was the last drink they would ever touch, and within hours many of them would lay dead, with the gully below running with their own blood.

8
REBELLION OR PREMEDITATED BLOODBATH?

Commissioner Robert Rede somehow had it in his head that the gold licence fees and their method of collection, had nothing to do with the diggers complaints. He believed them to be 'democratic nonsense'.

By Saturday evening the 2nd December 1854, Rede had at his disposal a sizeable military and police force in the government camp, with further reinforcements on the way from Melbourne. Already that day 256 reinforcements arrived from Melbourne, Geelong, and Castlemaine, which strengthened their force on the government camp to over 500 men. They consisted of mounted and foot police, military infantry, cavalry, with officers from the 12th, 40th and 99th regiments.

Just before dawn, John and his mates had nodded off to sleep around the fire, completely unaware of what was about to take place.

Rede had militarized 296 heavily armed men under the military command of Captain John Thomas of the 40th Somersetshire Regiment. There were:

> 65 men under Captain William Queade and Lieutenant William Paul of the 1/12th Suffolk Regiment;
>
> 87 men under Captain Henry Wise, Lieutenant George Bowdler, and Lieutenant Thomas Richards of the 1/40th Somersetshire Regiment;
>
> 30 mounted special forces cavalry under Lieutenant Charles Hall and Lieutenant William Gardiner of the 1/40th Somersetshire Regiment;
>
> 70 mounted Police under Sub Inspectors Hussey Chomley and Ladislaus Kossak;
>
> 24 foot police under Acting Sergeant William Fennelly of the 12th Regiment, along with Sub Inspectors Hussey Chomley and Ladislaus Kossak;
>
> 20 men of the 1/99th Lanarkshire Regiment consisting of 2 gun crews with two 6-pounder field guns/cannons;
>
> A further force of over two hundred soldiers and police under the command of Captain Arthur Atkinson of the 1/12th regiment, who were posted at the government camp to

protect the camp from any digger attack, while being available if reinforcements were needed.

Hotham had specifically sent the 40th regiment who were the elite special forces regiment with mounted infantry that could be mobilized at short notice and sent anywhere in the state. With a further 800 men already on their way along with two navy gun crews armed with two 6-pounders and two 12 pound howitzer canons, clearly this joint military force was not designed to simply keep the peace, but to annihilate the honest hard working Aussie diggers.

It was before dawn on Sunday 3rd December 1854. The fine mist rolling in through the cool crisp air of the gully, was fouled by the stench of premeditated mass murder being rolled out in military precision against the diggers.

These diggers were free settlers who emigrated to Australia for a better life. They were not soldiers, but Aussie miners from all walks of life, armed with nothing more than a handful of guns, pikes, swords and knives.

On the previous day there was up to 1,500 men in the stockade. Although word had come that the government would attack, nobody really believed it. John and many of his mates honestly believed the government would put an end to licence hunting due to their protesting.

These God fearing people believed if the government did attack, it certainly would not occur on the Sabbath, so many of them went off to their families.

Dalton's Gold
By Peter D Matthews

They were planning to go to Church this spine-chilling Sunday morning. Most of the Creswick diggers went off into town and never returned.

Sound asleep around the fire under the Southern Cross, John laid unaware that the gully below was flowing with red-toads and blue-pissants, lurking in the shadows, creeping slowly towards the diggers camp.

It was about 4:00am just as the sun was starting to rise, and the sky shone an eerie red glow towards the east, that John and his mates arose with a startle. All of a sudden horses were galloping at full tilt towards the stockade.

Was it friend or foe they thought as they waited to see the faces of the riders. Just at that point, a cry of 'Joe' came forward. The police detested being called 'blue-pissants' but tolerated being called 'Joe's'.

John could see the riders faces as they approached. It was Captain Henry Ross with the Independent Californian Rangers galloping towards the stockade. Captain Ross was screaming, 'The red-coats are upon us'.

As John looked up, there didn't seem to be any red-toads following him. But then he heard a loud crack. It was a single round fired from a rifle from one of the sentry posted near the Free Trade Hotel.

Lalor yelled the command, 'Californian Rangers to the front' just as they dismounted.

Carboni proved himself to be a gutless little traitor. He started running for his tent just outside the stockade, screaming, 'Every man for himself', then jabbered away in Italian.

John was fit and fast with his long legs. He grabbed Carboni on the shoulder demanding, 'Stay and fight like a man. You swore an oath like I did under the Southern Cross.'

Carboni struggled to get free, blurting 'I am not going to stand here and be slaughtered.'

John with a fully clenched fist, smacked Carboni right in the nose. He dropped him to the ground.

John was infuriated. His final word to Carboni was, 'Traitor'. In disgust John turned back to his mates while Carboni picked himself up and snuck through the timbers of the stockade to his tent.

The last time John saw Carboni, he was crouched down in front of his chimney to take protection from the gunfire, like a scared little girl in a storm. He was no Italian Revolutionary. He proved himself to be merely a vocal protester who in the end, deserted his mates.

Frederick Vern was a man after Carboni's own heart. He took off running into the scrub also deserting his mates.

John Thomas Dalton and his mates had sworn an oath under the Southern Cross, and this time he was not going to back away from the fight. He stood by Peter Lalor, waiting for the command.

It was 4:45am just upon day break with a blood red sky over the stockade, when they saw the red-toads and blue-pissants appear within 200-300m away. They were rising up out of the gully from the west.

John waited for the command from Lalor who seemed to hesitate. He seemed to be surveying the size of the force. Thinking they would stop and communicate, or at least read the riot act, he waited for Captain Thomas to send a messenger forward.

No messenger came. As they approached 200m from the stockade, John could see clearly the red-toads and blue-pissants in their uniforms. He could even see each of their faces.

In an instant they were surrounded with mounted police to the north, watching up the Melbourne Road to the east. The elite mounted special combat forces of the 40th regiment were posted to the south, to cut off any escape back to Ballarat. In from the west marched the foot police, and behind them, an overwhelming storming party of the 12th and 40th regiments.

John took notice of the uniforms, denoting their regiments. In true 40th regiment form, they wore their red single breasted shell jackets with bright pewter buttons with black leather shoulder straps, with pale brown cuffs to show they were the notorious 40th regiment. The 12th regiment wore yellow cuffs. The 40th regiment had blue oxford weave trousers with a scarlet welt down the outward length of the trousers while the 12th wore white linen to distinguish the different regiments to their commanders.[5]

John noticed their cheap English boots which were made from poor quality thick black leather which only covered the ankle. They had simply four eyelets which set them apart as rubbish in John's eyes. They were nothing like the quality boot he would make.

Although all wore the same blue wool Kilmarnock bonnet cap, each company had its own number and insignia, such as a brass bugle for the light infantry company with a green tuft, and a grenade for the grenadier company with a white tuft.[6]

They were well armed with either 1842 muskets with 60 rounds of ammunition on the belt along with a scabbard and bayonet; or a 33 inch spear pointed sword. The diggers were outnumbered, ill-equipped and relatively unprepared.

Many of them were believed to be Irish, but this is not true. John remembered distinctly that there were only about thirty Irish immigrants amongst the group. There were about twenty from Scotland; twenty or so from Canada or America, including the Independent Californian Rangers; about fifteen from other countries; and the rest were English or natural born Australians. All up, including the rangers, there were no more than 150 diggers in the stockade at the time of the attack. All of which moved to the goldfields of Victoria for a better life and raise a family. None of them expecting to be cut down in the fields of Ballarat like beasts.

The first shot was fired from the government forces. The diggers were astounded that no messenger came forward to negotiate. The diggers had no choice but fight or die.

The Independent Californian Rangers sent back a volley of return fire. In a crouched position behind a pile of slabs, John fired two rounds and hit nothing. John was fortunate enough to have a further two rounds left for his baby dragoon. Many of the diggers only had one or two rounds each. There were about seventy men with rifles, thirty with pistols, twenty with pikes, and thirty with swords and knives. All up there would not have been more than 200 rounds of ammo between the diggers.

Captain Ross guarded the north against the elite 40th regiment, while Thonen protected from the troopers coming in from the south. The pikemen under Michael Hanrahan and Patrick Curtain protected the east to Melbourne Road.

Lalor waits for the riot act to be read but instead bugles sounded from each of the flanks opposing the diggers as the blue-pissants and red-toads took their positions. The command 'charge' was heard as the 40th regiment and mounted police charged towards the stockade, sending a volley of fire throughout the camp.

The cavalry and troopers open fired on our forefathers as an act of war declared against the Australian public.

A full discharge of musketry from the military mowed down all who had their heads above the barricades. Ross was shot in the groin. Another shot struck Thonen exactly in the mouth which felled him on the spot. Those who suffered the most were the score of pikemen who stood their ground the whole time from when the division were posted at the top of the hill, facing the Melbourne Road from Ballarat. They were posted in double file under the slabs to stick the cavalry with their pikes. Hanrahan was there, although he was not mentioned in the history books. He stood his ground until Lalor made the call then retreated through the bush.

Lalor's division defended the south western side of the stockade, facing down the gully.

With the air thick with smoke and the deafening noise of musketry fire, confusion and disarray prevailed. The diggers could hardly see or hear what Lalor was shouting.

Lalor climbed the timbers protruding from a diggers hole and shouted, 'Pikeman come forward'.

Just at that fraction of a second, Lalor was hit in his left shoulder with a musket ball, along with two pistol rounds in his left arm. His arm was shattered and he dropped to the ground.

The red-coats broke through the stockade with ease. They shot and bayoneted every man that lay sprawled all over the ground. It did not seem to matter - they bayoneted the wounded and the dead - just to make sure.

The diggers put up one heck of a fight even unto death. Their valiant efforts could not save the Southern Cross. Unfortunately it was taken. The government force seemed to think it was some sort of sport, and the Southern Cross was their prize. A loud 'Hurrah' came with laughter from the red-toads.

This gave John an idea!

Lalor laid in the dirt, almost delirious from the pain. His final command was, 'Every man for himself' just as the infantry broke through the stockade.

John realized the red-coats and especially the troopers would kill Peter Lalor, so he planned his escape. He looked up and saw Lalor's timber shanty in front of him. He remembered the hole that he helped Peter dig under his shanty to store Lalor's gold.

'Give me a hand' John yelled to a couple of diggers nearby.

An Irish born digger and friend of Lalor's, named Thomas Gaynor, came to his rescue. He was the brother of Anne Duke who helped sew the Southern Cross flag.

The second fellow who came to help was an English born digger named James Ashburner.

John lifted Lalor's right shoulder trying to support his upper body, while the two other diggers grabbed his legs, and they headed for Lalor's shanty.

Gaynor protested, 'Are you bloody mad? They'll find him there and kill him for sure'.

'Trust me. You'll see' John asserted.

As they arrived at the entry of Lalor's shanty they laid Peter down just inside on the timber floor.

John said to Gaynor and Ashburner, 'Watch what I do, so you can place part of this floor back in afterwards, and then throw some slabs over the top of us. It will look like a timber store.'

John carefully removed part of the false floor and they lowered the body of Peter Lalor in. John jumped in the hole with Lalor. Gaynor and Ashburner threw the false floor back in with a few slabs of timber on top, then took off.

By this time many of the diggers had either escaped, been arrested or killed. Really is was the pikemen who were the unsung heroes, under the leadership of Hanrahan and Curtain, as they used their flimsy pikes against muskets to slow the advancement enough to allow John to hide Lalor away and let the others escape. Out of the twenty pikemen who took part in this incredible life and death struggle, only six survived to tell the tale of the Eureka Stockade.

The red-toads were rounding up prisoners. John could just see through the cracks in the floor and out the doorway.

John ripped his shirt off and used it as a tourniquet, placing it right up into Peter's armpit. As he began tightening it, Peter let out a deep moan because of the incredible pain.

Up came a stinking trooper with his blood stained blue shell jacket, with blood dripping all the way down to cover the white stripe on his blue trousers. His black four eyeleted cheap English boots were covered in a digger's blood.

He was well armed. He had a sword on his belt and a short 20 inch barrelled .65" Yeomanry 1844 pattern rifle in his hand.[7] This is the same short rifle used by Sergeants that John had seen with Commissioner Rede. The unusual thing though, was a .44 inch colt dragoon revolver tucked into his belt, which was not carried by other officers.

Dalton's Gold
By Peter D Matthews

The trooper walked into the shanty. A shiver ran down John's spine as he saw the face of the Trooper. It was Henry Goodenough who was supposed to be a digger. He was now dressed as a sergeant blue-pissant trooper.

John still had two rounds left. John just wanted to shoot him through the floor. Peter Lalor lay there looking and he too saw Goodenough, but Peter raised his right hand and grabbed John's trousers. He said nothing but shook his head to say, 'No. Don't it'.

John kept his cool and Goodenough left the shanty. On his way out, he thrust his bayonet into a deceased digger outside the shanty, thinking the whimper from Lalor had come from this poor fellow. He ripped into the carcass like a lion ripping into the flesh of its prey.

Ten minutes went by and the red-toads fell-in, before marching back to the government camp. Meanwhile the foulest deeds anyone has ever seen were being committed right there by the troopers and traps before John's very eyes. Angry and sickened by these atrocities, John wanted to kill every last one of them.

The troopers were the worst of the lot. They shot down anyone that ran away. They continued their murderous rampage by kicking, goring, shooting and even burning to death those that had laid down their arms in surrender. They gutted the injured with their bayonets and swords, spilling their blood and intestines all over the ground.

Dalton's Gold
By Peter D Matthews

All the tents in the vicinity were shot, then burnt. The most horrid sight was yet to come. One stinking Vandemonian trooper shot up a tent just beyond the stockade. The husband laid there almost dead and was not able to move. His wife was injured and screaming. The trooper dragged her body from the tent by her hair, then the most atrocious sight direct from the pit of hell, manifested itself. He used his spurs to contain her, lifted her dress, dropped his trousers and you can imagine the rest. This happened right in front of her dying husband.

It was too debased and deplorable to imagine a government employee doing such a thing, but yet it happened, right there in front of John Dalton.

John could not look any longer. He turned his head into the soil, quietly sobbing. Within minutes a single gunshot rang out. John wondered whether to even look up. After a few seconds he decided to lift his head. There laid the body of a woman silently still next to her now dead husband. She was shot after the dastardly deed, at point blank range and her brains splattered all over the place.

Out came a tin of turpentine. The trooper splashed it on tents, timbers, dead bodies and everything the diggers owned. Nothing was untouched. The entire area was soon alight. Even the shanty standing above Lalor and Dalton.

The red-toads had already departed, and the blue-pissants had just headed off, laughing and jeering, satisfied with their days work.

Dalton's Gold
By Peter D Matthews

It was time for John to make a run for it. He pushed up on the timbers but they were jammed tight. He thought to himself, 'I came to save my old mate but it looks like I've taken him to his grave'.

Lalor turned to John with a tear in his eye, 'Friend, you have fought well.'

Not even a second after the words came out of Lalor's mouth, the burning roof twisted and crashed backwards, dislodging the floor. John pushed the boards upwards and jumped out of the hole. He grabbed Lalor and dragged him out of the hole too.

John perched himself under Lalor's right arm and held him close. He walked him out into the scrub towards the east, away from the stockade to where the troopers couldn't find him.

John said to Peter, 'You stay here and I'll get Dr Carr'. John covered Peter Lalor in fallen branches to disguise him, just in case a blue-pissant came through the bush.

John headed back through the scrub to the stockade. Bodies lay everywhere and the gully literally flowing with blood. Everything was on fire. The smell of burning tents was choking, but what was worse, was the stench of burning flesh.

It looked like a war zone, and in fact it was. The Government of Victoria slaughtered over thirty Australian diggers, although only twenty-two were recorded. Amongst those were many innocent men and women whose bodies were burnt and never recorded.

Dalton's Gold
By Peter D Matthews

Those that died and were recorded, had a monument erected in their honour in 1886 at Eureka Park, Ballarat.

Lest we forget.

THE NAMES OF THE HERIOC DIGGERS WHOSE NAMES WERE RECORDED THAT DIED AS A RESULT OF THE MASSACRE

- William Emmerman, a Prussian born digger who laid down his life for his mates;
- Martin Diamond, an innocent Irish born shop owner shot by troopers in front of his wife as they burst into Diamond's Store looking for diggers;
- Thomas O'Neill, an Irish born pikeman, known for his valiance. With two broken legs and a musket ball in his body, he still held his pike and fought unto death for his mates;
- George Donaghey, an Irish born digger who laid down his life for his mates;
- George Clifton, an English born digger nicknamed "Happy Jack" died from multiple gunshot wounds defending his mates;
- Edward Quin, brother of John Quin, were two English brothers who emigrated from Lancashire to Australia for a better life;
- William Quinlan, an Australian born digger from Goulburn, NSW was cut down by red-toads defending his mates;
- Johann Hafele, from Württemberg, Germany, was the digger that handcrafted the pikes. He died with pike in hand defending his mates;
- John Crowe, an Irish born digger who came to Australia in search of gold to support his mother who was struggling to survive. He lived a simple life to send money back to his mother;

NAMES (CONTINUED FROM PREVIOUS PAGE)

- Thaddeus Moore, an Irish born digger who was shot during the battle and rescued by his brother Patrick Moore. He took his brother to Geelong to their sister and he died on the journey. He fought hard defending his mates;
- James Brown, an Irish born digger, died later of gunshot wounds defending his mates;
- James Ross, noted a Lieutenant Ross of the Independent Californian Rangers, defended the Southern Cross. He fought with every morsel of strength, unto death, defending his mates and the flag that they stood for;
- John Robertson, a Scottish born mate of Carboni, who was mistakenly believed to be Carboni fighting valiantly defending his mates unto death;
- Robert Fenton, an English born digger who died of gunshot wounds defending his mates;
- Edward McGlynn, an Irish born digger who died of gunshot wounds defending his mates;
- John Haynes was an Irish pikeman, also shot down defending his mates;
- Patrick Gittins, an Irish Creswick digger who came to defend his fellow diggers of Ballarat. He died with a pike in his hands;
- Michael Mullins, a relatively unknown Irish digger was shot dead defending his mates;
- Samuel Green, English born digger who was a close friend of Dalton. He died defending his mates, leaving behind his brother John and sister, Eliza;

NAMES (CONTINUED FROM PREVIOUS PAGE)

- Robert Julien, fellow Canadian from Nova Scotia, and friend of John Dalton. He was a digger who became an Independent Californian Ranger and fought valiantly but was shot and bayoneted by troopers. He died about a month after the massacre while John was at Smythesdale and John unfortunately missed his funeral;
- Edward Thonen, a Prussian born digger, was known as the 'lemonade man'. He was also a purveyor or grocer and became one of the leaders of the Ballarat Reform League. He died of multiple gunshot wounds to the face and mouth while defending his mates;
- John Hassel, misspelled as Hassle, was an English born digger, who died defending his mates.

LEST WE FORGET

9
RUN FOR YOUR LIFE

As he drew closer to the camp, John was overcome with the overwhelming stench of burning bodies causing him to stop and dry reach. The military did not collect or bury any of their victims bodies but only their own officers. Some of the diggers bodies were burnt. The rest were left sprawled all over the ground, like atrophy of their conquests.

The sight of women and children mourning the loss of husbands, fathers, and uncles mutilated bodies that lay sprawled right through the gully was something John could never forget. Beside them were their own weapons. It seemed like the government left them as a reminder to others to desist or face the same consequences.

John observed a printed notice stuck to the pole where the Southern Cross flag once was.

It read:

V. R.
NOTICE.
Government Camp,
Ballarat, Dec. 3rd, 1854.
Her Majesty's forces were this morning fired upon by a large body of evil-disposed persons of various nations, who had entrenched themselves in a stockade on the Eureka, and some officers and men killed. Several of the rioters have paid the penalty of their crime, and a large number are in custody.
All well-disposed persons are earnestly requested to return to their ordinary occupations, and to abstain from assembling in large groups, and every protection will be afforded to them by the authorities.
ROBT. REDE,
Resident Commissioner.
God save the Queen.[8]

    The notice was rather peculiar though. Rede could not have had time to set and print this notice after the massacre. It was not hand written, but a formal government notice that was printed on parchment by the Ballarat Times.
    That being the case, this notice was printed before the massacre took place, predetermining that

'some officers and men' would be killed. This confirmed John's suspicions, that Rede and Hotham were both involved in the premeditated strategy to massacre the diggers.

Those who were not killed or arrested, were forced to hide in fear of their lives. Many of the Aussie diggers that were familiar with the region and the local bushland, ran through the scrub for cover. Others ran back into town, only to be arrested.

Many of those arrested were shopkeepers and not in any way involved with the stockade.

One particular fellow from Creswick, named Henry Powell, was visiting a mate and his family at Ballarat. He stayed the night with them and had planned to depart later that morning.

William Cox heard noises outside his tent. He heard his mate Powell begging for mercy. This is his dying statement but I warn you, it is hard to handle:

> My name is Henry Powell. I am a digger residing at Creswick-creek. I left Creswick-creek about noon on Saturday, December 2nd. I said to my mates, 'You'll get the slabs ready. I will just go over to see Cox and his family at Ballarat.' I arrived at Ballarat about half-past four or thereabouts. I saw armed men walking about in parties of twenty or thirty; went to Cox's tent; put on another pair of trousers and walked down the diggings. I

looked in the stockade. After that, went home, went to bed in the tent at the back of Cox's tent, about half-past nine. On Sunday morning about four or half-past, was awoke by the noise of firing.
Got up soon after, and walked about twenty yards, when some trooper rode up to me. The foremost one was a young man whom I knew as the Clerk of the Peace [Akehurst].
He was of a light, fair complexion, with reddish hair. He told me to 'stand in the Queen's name! You are my prisoner.' I said "Very good, Sir". Up came more troopers. I cannot say how many. Believe about twenty or thirty. I said, 'Very well, gentlemen (!) don't be in a hurry, there are plenty of you', and then the young man struck me on the head with a crooked knife, about three feet and a half long, in a sheath. I fell to the ground. They then fired at me, and rode over me several times. I never had any hand in the disturbance. There, that's all.[9]

Henry Powell was only one innocent fellow who was recorded as being killed by the authorities. There were many more that John personally saw with his own eyes.

Dalton's Gold
By Peter D Matthews

John echoed, 'These atrocities by our own government were the worst I had ever seen or even heard of. No man should ever be subjected to what we were.'

One hundred and fourteen men were arrested and marched off to the government camp throughout the day. Carboni was one of them who was arrested later in the day, by Goodenough of all people. He believed Carboni was one of the ringleaders. In actual fact, Carboni was more of a vocal protestor, than a ringleader. He may have excited the men to action, but he was never involved in the battle.

Of the one hundred and fourteen men arrested, only twenty were born in Ireland; twelve from Scotland; three from America; two from Sweden; two from Italy; two from the Channel Islands off France; two from the Netherlands; one from Spain; and fourteen of unknown origin who were believed to be Australian.

The government assert that these diggers were from various nations, but predominantly Ireland. This was not the case. Half were from England or Australia. Those that emigrated prior to the gold rush of 1851 were classified as Australians as they emigrated to Australia to become Australians, not specifically during the gold rush.

Dalton's Gold
By Peter D Matthews

LIST OF PEOPLE ARRESTED AT EUREKA AND THEIR ORIGIN

Adams, Charles	England	Ellis, Joseph	England
Allen, Richard	Scotland	Fenwick, John	England
Alliare, Nicholas	Australia	Ferguson, Charles	USA
Anderson, Carl	Sweden	Fraser, Alexander	Scotland
Ashburner, James	England	Gilhooley, Patrick	England
Avondale, William	Australia	Gleeson, Michael	Ireland
Barry, Thomas	Ireland	Gray, Joseph	Scotland
Bazley, Henry	Australia	Hayes, Timothy	Ireland
Beattie, James	England	Hepburn, James	England
Bisk, Thomas	Australia	Hickey, Patrick	England
Box, Thomas	England	Hindon, Joseph	Australia
Brown, Charles	England	Hinds, Isaac	England
Bryan, William	England	Hogan, Jeremiah	Ireland
Burn, Edmund	England	Howard, Patrick	Ireland
Cahill, John	Ireland	Humphreys, Richard	England
Campbell, James	Scotland	James, Henry	England
Carboni, Raffaello	Italy	Joseph, John	USA
Cornish, Edwin	England	Keddar, Charles	Australia
Cornish, John	England	Kelly, John	USA
Cornish, Richard	England	Kennedy, Michael	Ireland
Cornish, Thomas	England	Kennedy, Patrick	Ireland
Davidson, George	Scotland	Kent, Francis	England
Degan, Thomas	Australia	Kinnear, Martin	England
Delamere, John	Australia	Leadow, John	Australia
Develin, William	Australia	Leslie, Robert	Scotland
Dignum, Thomas	Australia	Livingstone, Charles	Australia
Dynan, Michael	Australia	Mackeon, Joseph	Scotland
Edwards, John	Scotland	Manning, John	Ireland

Dalton's Gold
By Peter D Matthews

LIST OF PEOPLE ARRESTED AT EUREKA AND THEIR ORIGIN (continued)

Name	Origin	Name	Origin
Mayher, Thomas	Ireland	Sheedy, Patrick	Ireland
McCartney, Daniel	Scotland	Smith, Arthur	Ireland
McInnes, Duguld	Scotland	Somerville, William	Scotland
McMahon, Edward	Australia	Sorenson, Jacob	Australia
Meade, Patrick	Ireland	Stafford, William	England
Molloy, William	Ireland	Steer, William	England
Murphy, Thomas	Ireland	Swanson, Andrew	Sweden
O'Brien, Kennedy	Ireland	Thompson, George	England
Orr, Matthew	England	Tighe, Thomas	Australia
Pardy, John	Australia	Trynon, Henry	Australia
Penny, Samuel	Australia	Tuohey, Michael	Ireland
Penrose, Joseph	England	Vennik, Jan	Netherlands
Pergo, ?	Spain	Walker, Joseph	England
Peters, Cornelius	Netherlands	White, Andrew	England
Phelan, John	Ireland	Winkfield, Robert	England
Pohl, Adolph	Australia	Winkley, William	England
Powell, John	England	Wright, William	England
Priaulx, Peter	Channel Islands		
Quin, John	Ireland		
Reid, Henry	Australia		
Robilliard, Henry	Channel Islands		
Rodan, John	Australia		
Romeo, Francis	Italy		
Ross, Alexander	Scotland		
Ryan, Martin	Ireland		
Ryley, Walter	Australia		
Sexton, James	Australia		

SUMMARY - COUNTRY OF ORIGIN

Australia	24
Channel Islands	2
England	32
Ireland	20
Italy	2
Netherland	2
Scotland	12
Spain	1
Sweden	2
USA	3
Unknown (Aust?)	14
TOTAL	114

Dalton's Gold
By Peter D Matthews

The author has traced every person on the list to find their origin and immigration papers, which confirmed that John Dalton and Peter Lalor were correct - The government fired upon, indiscriminately killing their own people. They committed premeditated mass murder in the name of keeping the peace. This was caused in the first place by a haemorrhaging government purse, where the government under Charles Hotham, used military force to collect his disproportionate but compulsory taxes.

A number of other historians attribute the fact of Thomas O'Rourke and Herman Steinman were amongst those arrested.[10] However Thomas O'Rourke only arrived in Australia on 6 June 1857, and Herman Steinman arrived 2 February 1860, therefore neither were present during the Eureka stockade in 1854.

Alexander Fraser, a Scottish born digger on the list was also charged and fined for calling out 'Joe' who warned the diggers that the blue-pissants and red-toads were coming.

Martial Law

On Monday 4th December 1854, Governor Hotham declared Martial Law, under the recommendation of Commissioner Rede.

Two days after the massacre, some 800 troops from all over the state arrived at Ballarat, along with a naval contingent from HMS Electra and HMS Fantome with two more 6-pounder field guns and two 12 pounder howitzer canons.[11] They were despatched by Hotham days earlier. They were the forces the diggers had heard were on their way from Melbourne.

Major General Sir Robert Nickle commanded the force. He was surprised to walk amongst the people of Ballarat without any fear whatsoever. He reported this to Hotham and within days Martial Law was repealed on the 9th December 1854.

In typical blue-pissant form, they prepared depositions (statements) against those in custody from officers involved in the massacre, along with spies in the camp. These depositions, although biased, were used as evidence against the diggers.

The evidence was heard by EPS Sturt, the Ballarat magistrate, who took over from D'Ewes. Of the one hundred and fourteen arrested, only thirteen were charged with high treason and committed to trial.

Three men from America were arrested: Charles Derius Ferguson, John Kelly and John Joseph. After the intervention of Dr Kenworthy, who was an American doctor on the goldfields, along with James Tarleton from the American Consulate, two of the men were released without charge. They were Charles Derius Ferguson and John Kelly, who were both Caucasian Americans.

The third man, John Joseph, was an uneducated African American. He was left in gaol by the American government, charged with high treason.

The thirteen men were Timothy Hayes, Raffaello Carboni, John Joseph, James Beattie, James Campbell,

Dalton's Gold
By Peter D Matthews

John Manning, William Molloy, John Phelan, Henry Reid, Michael Tuohey, Thomas Dignum, Jacob Sorenson and Jan Vennik (miss-spelled as Vennick).

The rest of the 114 arrested were released due to a lack of evidence.

Lalor, Black and Vern could not be found. So Hotham offered a reward of £200 each for Black and Lalor, and £500 for Frederick Vern.

Run and Hide

John had no shirt on, and the rest of his body was covered in blood. He had to find some clothes before walking into town, otherwise he would be arrested with the others.

He headed down the gully away from town, to his camp at Dalton's Flat. He washed up and changed his clothes to his Sunday best, along with his fancy dress boots. While he was there, he grabbed a couple of pair of new boots that he had recently finished for customers, and walked into town.

Up strode a Vandemonian trooper enquiring, 'Wot's ya name, mate? Were you at the stockade?'

'No Sir. I am a boot maker from Smythesdale. I'm here to deliver these boots to my customers at Ballarat' John cleverly replied.

This allowed John free access throughout the camp to visit his customers, and deliver his boots without question.

John headed to the hospital to see Margaret and find Dr Carr, to take him back to Peter Lalor. Fortunately

Dalton's Gold
By Peter D Matthews

Margaret was at the hospital. She was attending the wounded, but frantic for news of John. When each body was brought in, she wound race in to see if it were the body of her new husband.

John walked into the room while whistling. Upon seeing Margaret, he exclaimed, 'Hello my love? Whatever has happened?'

He did this for the benefit of the other employees in the hospital, allowing them to think he was not actually there in the stockade. Otherwise word would get out to Rede and he would be arrested too.

Margaret raced to John and grabbed him tight. She sighed, 'I'm so happy you're safe. So you were not in the stockade when the road coats attacked?'

'No love, I was out at Smythesdale last night. I only came to Ballarat this morning to deliver these boots to my customers' John squeaked.

Seeing a little blood on the side of John's neck, Margaret licked her finger and wiped it clean. She said nothing as she knew there were spies in their midst.

'Where's your Uncle?' John enquired.

'He's out tending the wounded' Margaret hinted, while pointing over to a shop.

John quietly confirmed, 'I'll catch up with him later. I've got to go, but I will be back later for you'.

John headed over to the store that Margaret pointed out. He was busy trying to save the life of a digger who was riddled with bayonet wounds. The poor digger had everything laid out on the shop counter, which was used as a makeshift surgeon's table.

Dalton's Gold
By Peter D Matthews

John hollered, 'Dr Carr, I need you to come to one of my friends who needs help'.

Dr Carr barked at John, 'I have enough to do right now. Can't you see, boy! You will just have to wait.'

John waited impatiently, tapping his foot on the floor in protest. He was not the type of person to just sit there, especially when he knew his mate needed his urgent help.

'I'll be back soon. I'd better go and check on him' John uttered.

He headed back to the scrub area that he had left Peter Lalor. He could clearly see the branches where he laid Peter but all he could find was a trail of blood.

'Oh no', John thought to himself. 'I hope the blue-pissants haven't found him.'

John followed the blood trail to the store of Stephen and Jane Cumming, just beyond the stockade. They were near George and Phoebe Emmerson's store.

John walked in and there was Stephen over the body of Peter Lalor, trying to bandage his arm.

'Is he all right? I left him out in the scrub to get help. I came back for him and he was gone. All I found was a blood trail which scared the life out me' John fearfully asked.

Rather concerned, Stephen echoed John's fears, 'He's in bad shape and needs help. Jane and Phoebe have gone across the gully to the Presbytery to see Father Smyth. He can't stay here.'

George Scobie walked out from the rear of Emmerson's store. He came up from behind John with a pistol in his hand, aimed at directly at John's back. As George approached, he blurted, 'Dalton, it's you. I thought it was a blue-pissant spy and I was about to drop him.'

John nervously sputtered, 'I have been to see Dr Carr and he is coming as soon as he finishes fixing up another digger'.

Scobie whispered to John, 'Phoebe and Jane went to get help to move him to Father Smyth at the Presbytery. I hid here, along with Humffray and Black. Phoebe hid us away while the troopers came in looking for us. I decided to stay to protect Phoebe and George from these murderous mongrels.'

'All right then. You and Stephen get him over to the Presbytery and I will get Dr Carr there as soon as I can. He's tending a digger with bayonet wounds just up the road' John agreed.

He headed back to Dr Carr who was just about finished. John nervously told Dr Carr that his friend was Peter Lalor, and he was still alive, but had his left arm shattered by three gunshot wounds and it was almost hanging off.

Arriving at the Presbytery just after dark, Lalor was conscious but had lost a lot of blood. Dr Carr looked over the wounds and moved the arm around to see what damage had occurred.

Dr Carr said, 'The humerus and tubercle were smashed by the musket ball. Hmmm, there doesn't seem to be lot of options here.'

Peter Lalor heckled, 'My humour has always been damaged', in an effort not to lose his sense of humour.

Dr Carr, with a fearful but stern look upon his face, asserted, 'The humerus is also broken down further in several places. It's almost disintegrated. We have no choice but amputate.'

John was really concerned upon hearing the word 'amputate'. He jumped in, 'Surely there must be some other way'.

'I'm sorry, but I can see no other way. If we don't amputate, he won't last the night. I'll need a team of surgeons. Dr Doyle is the best surgeon on the goldfields. I will send for him and Dr Stewart' Dr Carr insisted.

Dr Carr asked Father Smyth to send for Dr Doyle and Dr Stewart along with Mrs Carr, who was his nurse.

Meanwhile Dr Carr prepared Lalor for surgery. John helped by dragging an old wooden table into the middle of the dimly lit room. This was the operating table. He placed linen on the table, like making a bed with sheets and blankets.

With the help of Father Smyth, Anastasia Hayes and Tobias McGrath, John and Dr Carr lifted Peter Lalor onto the makeshift operating table.

Alongside the wooden operating table was a slim inclined timber pulpit, which was placed ready for the surgeon's instruments.

The old feeble lantern had hardly enough light to read, let alone to operate under. Candlesticks were gathered and placed around the operating table to light up the room.

Dr Carr told Father Smyth, 'You can hold the bowl' as he handed him a white enamelled round metal bowl.

Father Smyth put out his hand to receive the bowl and just nodded sheepishly, without saying a word.

By the time Dr Carr had the makeshift operating theatre ready, Dr Doyle and Dr Stewart arrived. Dr Doyle looked over the wounds and just shook his head.

Lalor piped up, 'This is your best surgeon! He is no older than me? How old are you lad?'

'I am 29 years old and one of few properly registered surgeon's in this Victorian Colony' articulated Dr Timothy Doyle with his strong Kilkenny accent.

'Oh, you're Irish' Lalor responded with a sigh of relief.

'What about your assistant?' Lalor added.

'I am Dr James Stewart. I am not his assistant. I am 24 years of age but have a perfect steady hand and a surgeon in my own right' the offended Dr Stewart complained.

His long finely featured face made him look a lot younger than he really was.

With all the pleasantries over and blood still seeping from Lalor's arm, the amputation took place.

Dr Doyle was handed the handsaw, but he hesitated for a moment. Father Smyth handed the bowl to Anastasia Hayes as his stomach just couldn't handle it.

Lalor yelled at Dr Doyle, 'Come on lad, courage, courage, lop it off!'

Dr Doyle grabbed a handkerchief and a small bottle of ether. This is all they had as anaesthetic in those days. He poured a small amount on the handkerchief and placed it over Lalor's mouth and asked Lalor to, 'breathe in deeply for me'. Within a couple of minutes Lalor was out cold.

Before long the surgery was over and the blood flow stopped. John helped carry Lalor into Father Smyth's bed where he slept for the rest of the night.

John took three bags of blood soaked linen to burn off, along with the amputated arm which Father Smyth insisted on having a proper burial. John burnt the sheets down in the gully to remove any evidence. Merely throwing them out could alert the government that Peter Lalor could still be alive. Many thought he was already dead but his body was never confirmed amongst those killed or burnt.

With his mate Tobias McGrath, John buried the severed arm of Peter Lalor. They gave the arm a proper burial just as Father Smyth insisted, down a deep mineshaft that was no longer used.

John went back to the Presbytery and sat by Peter Lalor the entire night.

Father Smyth feared the government would come due to some neighbouring spies. The lights had been on all night with doctors coming and going. This

Dalton's Gold
By Peter D Matthews

would no doubt raise suspicions. At dawn Peter Lalor awoke and Father Smyth asked if Peter knew anyone that could look after him because he couldn't stay at the presbytery.

Lalor, although still a bit groggy, confirmed, 'I'll be right. I've got a mate at Warrenheip who will look after me until I get back onto my feet.'

Father Smyth prepared his horse while Lalor gathered his few belongings.

John happily offered, 'If you run into trouble, then make sure you come and visit me at Smythesdale. I am going to start a boot makers shop there, near the Court House Hotel. You are always welcome in our tent.'

Father Smyth dressed Lalor in his priest's clothes and helped him up onto the horse. Lalor rode off gently into the ranges, headed for Warrenheip which was just south east of Ballarat.

Peter Lalor never went back for his gold. John went back to retrieve it for him, before going through to Smythesdale. Insead John found the hole had been cleaned out completely. There was not a thing left in the hole - only blood stained soil. It seemed as though the blue-pissants came back searching for Lalor, and took everything of value along the way.

John called past the transport business of George Scobie asking if he could transport them and their belongings to Smythesdale? George agreed, 'I'll be over to your camp with the dray in half an hour'.

John and Margaret went back to Dalton's Flat to pack their belongings and dig up what gold he had left.

Dalton's Gold
By Peter D Matthews

The flat bottomed wagon was hitched with two strong Clydesdale horses. John and George loaded all John's belongings onto the dray, while Margaret carefully loaded her own.

Arriving in Smythesdale that afternoon, they pitched a tent near the old Court House Hotel on the main road, which is now called Brooke Street.

In those days, Smythesdale was called "Smythes" after Captain John Smythe, who was a pastoralist in the region.

By December 1854, Smythesdale was a bustling, thriving community of almost 5,000 people. Most of whom were diggers who worked along the Woady Yaloak Creek.

Smythesdale was surrounded with the natural beauty of picturesque ranges, covered with white gum, stringy bark, with the odd blackwood and swamp sheoak trees.

The forest was teaming with wildlife such as kangaroos, wallabies, koalas, possums, bandicoots, but the most interesting to the diggers was the wild turkeys that were prolific through the region.

Not long after they pitched their tent, up walked a wild turkey into the camp. John grabbed it around the neck and asked a nearby digger if it was his.

The neighbour chuckled, 'Na mate, they're wild. Looks like you caught dinner already.'

Margaret grabbed the wild turkey from John. She insisted, 'Give it to me. I know how to cook turkey.' Off she went preparing it for dinner.

Dalton's Gold
By Peter D Matthews

Many attribute the founders of Smythesdale to be John Lynch who was a digger of Ballarat. However, this is not true as John Lynch didn't move to Smythesdale until a few months later in 1855. This was well after the Dalton's settled in Smythesdale.

They also attribute John Lynch as assisting hiding Peter Lalor. This is also not true as John Lynch ran from the stockade before Lalor and Dalton were hidden. This is why in his book entitled, 'The Story of the Eureka Stockade', that he couldn't write a detailed account of what happened. This is because, he simply wasn't there.

John Lynch was later arrested down the main street of Ballarat. An officer believed he saw him earlier that day in the stockade but it was soon thrown out of court, due to a lack of evidence on the part of the arresting officer.

A 'wild turkey' is how John Dalton described John Lynch - a madman, obsessed with the theory of mining, running around in all directions, rather than actually digging in a hole to find gold.

A few days after they settled in at Smythesdale, George Scobie arrived on his dray, along with what looked like Father Smyth with him.

The fellow with George Scobie was wearing priest's attire, but seemed much taller than Father Smyth. 'Could it be Peter Lalor', he questioned?

He was wearing a large black bell topper hat, like Father Smyth, but with a white handkerchief over his nose and mouth to hide his face.

Dalton's Gold
By Peter D Matthews

By this time John realized it was Peter Lalor as he was having trouble getting himself down from the front of the dray, so John ran over to help him down.

Peter confirmed, 'I couldn't stay in Warrenheip. My mate wasn't there and his wife allowed me to stay but then disappeared off to Ballarat. I suspected she was going to inform the blue-pissants and thought it prudent to leave.'

'You can stay here with us' John blurted without even thinking.

'No. The blue-pissants will hunt me down and cart you away too. Hide me away in a hole, just for few days, until I am well enough to go to be with Alicia, my Fiancé' Peter begged.

'I know just the place' John suggested.

By this time it was late afternoon and Margaret shared what food she had prepared with Peter and George. George headed off early the next morning and John took Peter down to an old abandoned mineshaft, not far from his camp.

John and Margaret looked after Peter Lalor for over a week. They lowered food down to him just on dusk every afternoon.

Blue-pissants had poured into the region looking for Frederick Vern. Someone had reported that Vern was seen in Smythesdale wearing women's clothing.

The blue-pissants were searching every tent and every hole, after all there was a five hundred pound bounty on his head. Lalor was just as sought after with a two hundred pound bounty on his head, especially with posters all down the main street of Smythesdale, describing Lalor to a tee.

The only way to smuggle Lalor out, was at night. John sent word to Ballarat, asking for George Scobie to cart his 'precious cargo' to Geelong.

However Scobie was not due back for days and Lalor couldn't wait as the authorities were closing in on his whereabouts.

John went by horse personally to Ballarat hoping to find someone who would transport Lalor through the treacherous journey at night.

John went to the shop of Anastasia Hayes in the hope that she could help. Meanwhile Timothy Hayes was locked up in a prison cell accused of high treason.

Just then Patrick Carroll called in. He dropped off a small package to them from Geelong. Patrick and his sons operated a transport business to and from Geelong. Anastasia invited him to the back room where John Dalton was.

'How can I help?' Patrick asked. He was thinking there may have been an inappropriate load of tobacco or sly grog to bring in from Geelong.

'How much would you charge me to take someone to Geelong at night?' John hesitantly questioned.

Patrick realising the request from a back room meant that this person must be one of the three who were wanted by the law 'dead or alive'.

'Thirty pounds for freight like that' Patrick informed. If he was going to cart a fugitive, at least he would do well out it for his trouble.

"I'll give you fifty pounds if you deliver this letter to a lady at Geelong and bring back a response, then next trip take my mate back to her at Geelong. I'll give you ten now; twenty on pickup of my mate; and twenty next time you come through, once I know he is safe. Agreed?' John forcefully asserted.

'Who is it that I am taking this letter to, and may I ask before I commit my family to doing this, who is your friend?' Patrick asked.

'Understand me clearly - if you repeat this to anyone, I will find you and I will kill you. If I don't, there will be others who will. The letter is going to Miss Alicia Dunne, assistant teacher of St Mary's School in Geelong. She is the fiancé of my mate, Peter Lalor' John announced with a serious look on his face, while he put his hand on his pistol just in case.

Patrick laughed, 'I know Alicia. She is the daughter of a mate of mine, Patrick Dunne. If you had told me that earlier you it was Lalor you were talking about, I would have done the job for half the price. I have been carted grog from Geelong to Ballarat for Lalor for months.'

John gratefully handed Patrick the letter and ten pounds. He thought it best to offer him a reasonable sum. Otherwise he could turn Lalor in for the two hundred pound reward. Friend or not, this sort of money could tempt just about any man, but not Patrick Carroll. He was man of honour.

'Bring your cargo here for pick up just before dawn on Sunday 17th December and I will pick him up from here. Do not be late.' Patrick added.

Patrick Carroll arrived just before sunrise just as he promised. With him was his two sons, John and Michael. On one of the drays, he had a small load of timber and next to it, a pine box.

Peter walked out towards the dray with Patrick's two sons sheltering him from sight.

'I'm not dead yet' Peter exclaimed, when he saw the pine coffin on the back of the dray.

'It's the best way to transport you, with no questions asked' Patrick replied.

Michael and John Carroll helped Peter into the coffin and closed the lid, loosely nailing it shut. The side facing the timbers had holes to allow Lalor to breathe but Lalor still wasn't happy about it.

Just as Patrick and his sons were leaving, Patrick turned to John and questioned, 'Didn't you just marry Dr Carr's daughter?'

John defensively scoffed, 'Margaret is my wife but thankfully she is not Dr Carr's daughter. She is his niece.'

Patrick looked at John quite puzzled, blurting out, 'How could you be mates with Lalor, and will pay to smuggle him away, but are related to that conniving doctor who is a special constable of Rede.'

Dalton's Gold
By Peter D Matthews

Patrick's long thin face dropped. He realized he had let the cat out of the bag. John's face changed immediately the words came out of Patrick's mouth. He was already angry with Dr Carr but had no idea that Dr Carr was a Special Constable for Commissioner Rede.

The tone of John's voice changed as he insisted, 'Lalor is my mate and I vowed to protect him. I was not there during the attack - understand.'

Concealing his rage, he continued, 'However, Dr Carr is a relative by marriage, not by choice. What is this about him being a Special Constable for Rede?'

'Didn't you know?' Patrick uttered surprisingly.

'No, keep going. I want to hear exactly what you know and how you know it' John demanded.

'Back in October last year, I was in the government camp delivering goods and I saw Dr Carr being sworn in as a Special Constable. After the attack I was delivering goods to government camp again. It was just after first light and Dr Carr was there treating soldiers. I saw this with my own eyes and could not believe it, but Dr Carr asked an officer for a corner of the Southern Cross flag as a memento and they ripped a corner off it and gave it to him' Patrick mumbled, in a rather terrified tone. He didn't want to be the one who told John, but he was just as concerned that John could shoot him right there in front of his children.

He noticed John's revolver in his belt and in a fearful tone pleads, 'Please, I am here helping you. I thought you knew?'

A sigh of relief came over Patrick as John conceded, 'Thank you for telling me and thank you again for your help today. I will see you upon your return for the balance of the money.'

'I must be off' Patrick gasped. He certainly didn't want to stick around after dropping that clanger.

The Carroll boys camped out by day and drove by night in order to avoid the authorities. Peter arrived safely in Geelong and stayed for many months tucked away in the Young Queen Hotel. The hotel owner, Edward Walford, was a good friend of Patrick Dunne's, Alicia's father. Edward took care of Peter like he was family during the time he was there.

The first operation by the Ballarat surgeons was not quite a success as they left a fragment of bullet in Peter's stump. He had a second operation at the Young Queen Hotel which was paid for by Patrick Dunne and Edward Walford.

Meanwhile the thirteen diggers were laid up in despicable conditions in the police lock-up, having all been charged with high treason.

John's fury burned as he considered what to do with Dr Carr. Should he avenge his mates? And if so, how?

Dalton's Gold
By Peter D Matthews

10
REVENGE - A TWO EDGED SWORD

Mourning or revenge was the topic of the day. Should the diggers run and hide or should they continue to stand against the tyrannous government?

John, having mourned for his mates, now set his sights directly on Dr Carr as he contemplated revenge. His fury burned inside him. He was set on avenging his mates. But John was a level headed man, unlike Dr Carr. Patience was a virtue John had plenty of, and instead he sat back quietly in the shadows, waiting for the perfect moment.

John struggled for weeks with the thought of Dr Carr conspiring with Rede. He remembered how Dr Carr had asked John to keep Margaret safe at the hospital. He must have known full well that the government were planning to massacre the diggers. Dr Carr knew that John could quite easily have been one of the deceased. He also would have known that the only way Hotham and Rede could legally annihilate the diggers, was if they picked up arms against the government.

    John had tried to talk to Lalor and his mates about laying down their arms. All of sudden, it dawned on John suddenly that Dr Carr was used by Rede to plant the thoughts of the government attack, giving them no option but defend. One way they would be slaughtered if they picked up arms, and the other if they laid down their arms, they were defenceless. Either way they were snookered and Dr Carr was used as the messenger of destruction.

    Again and again Dr Carr had betrayed John, and even Margaret as his own blood. John had known that Dr Carr was a government spy, but the thought of him being sworn in a Special Constable directly against the diggers, was something John just couldn't tolerate. It left such a foul taste in John's mouth that it couldn't be ignored.

    John had made his decision: revenge was the only option. He did not want to kill Dr Carr but banish him away, so that he was never seen again on the Ballarat goldfields.

    John had decided to go to Geelong to pick up supplies for his new shoe shop. He hitched a ride with Patrick Carroll on his dray. While sitting around the campfire the first night, John posed the question, 'Do you know anyone on the docks that could organise for someone being taken back to England in shackles?'

    Patrick looked at John's resolve and knew that he was serious.

'I gather you are talking about Dr Carr? I do know someone but how are you going to get him on the ship?' Patrick asked.

John smiled, 'You leave that to me. If I can get him on a ship just before departure, can you organise it with the right dockman and the ship's captain to keep him in chains the entire journey?'

'I'll talk to a mate of mine on the docks and see what I can do' Patrick agreed.

Dr Carr was a well hated man, and Patrick Carroll was one of them. He had many a run-ins with Dr Carr when he was delivering goods to the hospital, so was happy to assist.

After John picked up the leather that he had been waiting on, Patrick strode up, 'There's someone I want you to meet'.

Patrick took John back to side of the dock to meet a short but shrewd little Irish fellow who would not be named, other than, 'Michael the dockman'. He was no more than 150cm tall, with a rounded red face, overshadowed by long curly whiskers.

With a pipe in the side of his mouth, he uttered, 'So you want to smuggle an unsavoury person back to England? That can be done but it will cost you. I have to pay the captain and the crew. And I have to feed my family of seven children.'

Whether he had seven children or not was questionable but it seemed like a justifiable excuse to ask for an exorbitant fee.

John confirmed, 'I will bring him here to meet his brother on an incoming ship. You tell me the ship and I will book his brother a ticket to come and escort him back home. When we arrive, you take him below and shackle him in and gag him of course. Then you take his brother below while he is foaming at the mouth, and he will think he has lost his mind. Keep him there the entire journey and free him once he arrives in England.'

'No problem' the dockman belched. 'That will be a hundred pound.'

'Agreed. When do you want him here' John asked.

'I know just the ship. I'll send word through Patrick here, when I know their next departure and arrival date. You come with the fellow, but don't forget the hundred pound' Michael the dockman added.

Michael the dockman put out his hand in agreement. John shook his hand firmly and nodded, confirming the gentleman's agreement.

Within weeks of arriving back at Smythesdale, Patrick arrived with a note from Michael the dockman from Geelong. The note was:

'Board ship in Liverpool. James Baines to
arrive Geelong late February 1855.'

Great, John thought, and wrote a letter to Dr Carr's brother in England:

I am John Thomas Dalton, husband of Margaret Carr, daughter of William. Your brother Dr Alfred Carr, has fallen ill and is not of sound mind. I know you are a

busy man running the store but could you please come on the ship, James Baines to Geelong. It is due to arrive here in February 1855. I need you to accompany him home to England on the return journey? Please find enclosed the fair.
    Yours Truly
    J.T.Dalton
    Ballarat, Colony of Victoria

    Frederick sent a letter back confirming that his wife, Mrs Carr, would visit instead of him because he was too busy working his merchant business.
    In the meantime John had word from Patrick Carroll that Michael the dockman had requested they be on the dock for the ship's departure at 8:00am sharp, next Thursday morning. So John sent a note to Dr Carr at the Ballarat hospital:

    Dr Carr
    I have just heard news from your brother, Frederick Carr, enclosed. His wife is planning to visit and will be arriving on the ship James Baines, at 8:00am on Thursday and requests you meet her upon arrival. I will come and meet you on Tuesday morning to accompany you to Geelong.
    Yours Truly
    J.T. Dalton

    John rode in Tuesday morning to Ballarat and picked up Dr Carr and they both headed off for Geelong.

Dalton's Gold
By Peter D Matthews

In a whirlwind of excitement, Dr Carr chatted all the way to Geelong about the family back in England and Ireland. He was like a little school boy waiting to go to school to play with his mates. John almost felt regretful for what he had planned. Never had he seen Dr Carr so happy and excited. It was almost like he was a different man.

Dr Carr's father was Captain Carr of the 3rd Buffs Foot Regiment of East Kent. This was the first time John had heard that his wife's grandfather was a red-coat!

Captain Carr served in East India, where Dr Carr and his brothers were born. However his father had passed away in 1845. William Carr met his Irish bride and they moved to Birr, Tipperary, Ireland. While the rest of the family moved back to England.

Captain Carr was from Kent. Dr Carr and his brothers were born in East India to a red-toad father and an Irish mother. 'Wow' John thought, 'I had no idea'. He only knew that Margaret was from Tipperary and had assumed the rest of the family were from Tipperary.

John also learned that Dr Carr had another brother besides William and Frederick, named Edward. Neither Dr Carr or Margaret had ever talked about Edward before.

Frederick lived with Dr Carr's mother at 6 Peel Terrace, Heaton Chapel. Heaton Chapel was a small English village just a few kilometres outside the centre of Manchester, in the north of England. It is now called Stockport.

Dalton's Gold
By Peter D Matthews

Upon arriving at the dock, Michael the dockman was there, right on time at 8:00am. The ship was ready to depart. All the goods were stored below deck, and they were ready to set sail.

The captain of the ship came down the gangway and in a big voice bellowed, 'You must be here to see Mrs Carr. She is waiting in my cabin. Come help get her luggage below.'

'Is she sick? I am a surgeon, if she needs help' Dr Carr declared. He was concerned that if his sister-in-law was in the captain's cabin, she may have been in need of medical attention.

'She is a little weak' the Captain hinted.

John accompanied Dr Carr and the captain below deck. It was extremely dark with only a faint light in the distance. Dr Carr bumped into a big burly Scottish sailor and all of sudden the burly Scotsman and five other sailors grabbed Dr Carr.

They dragged him backwards quickly to the side of the ship and shackled him to the hull.

'What is the meaning of this? Unshackle me now, you filthy swine. Where is my sister-in-law? Is my brother behind this?' Dr Carr ranted, as his eyes began to adjust.

The burly Scotsman stuck a handkerchief in Dr Carr's mouth to keep him quiet.

John stepped forward and confessed, 'Your brother is not here. You're going to be taken back to England and you'd better not return. You betrayed me and even your own blood, Margaret. You were sworn in as a Special Constable and now I know why. Because your father, as you admitted, was a Captain of the red-toads - the same red-toads that slaughtered my mates. You knew Rede could only attack if they found us with arms in our hands. You conspired with Rede to slaughter us diggers. You turned your back on me, hoping I would be killed with my mates. Now I'm going to turn my back on you. If you return I'll kill you myself.'

Dr Carr in a psychotic tone, spat the handkerchief out just as Mrs Carr walked in. He was foaming at the mouth and screaming at the top of his lungs. She ran out of the stow hold absolutely terrified.

Dr Carr screamed at the Captain, 'Unshackle me now or when we get to England, I will have you arrested'.

The captain laughed at Dr Carr. Instead he turned to the Scottish sailor chuckling, 'He's yours, because I know how much you hate him'.

Dr Carr was well known amongst many of the ship's crews. Nobody wanted to work with him and particularly this one big burly Scottish sailor who had sailed with Dr Carr before.

'You're my bitch now for the entire journey' the Scotsman excitedly blurted. He took great joy in stuffing the handkerchief back in Dr Carr's mouth and tied it securely with a rope around his head. Then he threw a bedpan of stale urine over Dr Carr's face. He was amused and excited with given the pleasure of looking after Dr Carr.

Dalton's Gold
By Peter D Matthews

John turned to Michael the dockman and gave him the one hundred pound. He echoed, 'By the looks of this, it is going to be an interesting trip?'

Turning to the Scotsman, John gave him an extra twenty pound, taunting, 'Make sure you take extra care of him.'

'Oh, I will. Thank you, Sir' replied the keyed up Scotsman.

John headed out to meet Margaret's aunt. John smiled, 'Hi, I'm John Dalton, husband of Margaret. I'm sorry you had to see him in this state. He needs help. The captain will keep him restrained and look after him during the journey. Don't worry, you'll be safe.'

The call came from the captain for the ship to depart so John bid her farewell, hoping for an uneventful journey home.

One can only imagine what horrid and detestable things the Scotsman did to Dr Carr on the way back to England.

Covered in the stench or alcohol and urine, Dr Carr alighted the ship at the Liverpool dock, vowing to have the captain arrested.

Dr Carr ran from the ship, straight to the Liverpool Courthouse and demanded the Captain of the ship be charged for restraining him in chains the entire journey. He completely ignored Mrs Carr, believing she was in on the whole thing.

Meanwhile, John arrived back at Ballarat and learned that Dr Carr was required in Melbourne to testify in court as a witness for Raffaello Carboni. He suddenly realized that his plan for revenge was like a two edged sword - although it dealt with one problem, there was other unforeseen consequences.

John told Anastasia Hayes what happened, and asked her to get word to her husband Timothy Hayes, who was also in gaol with Carboni. Carboni never spoke to John Dalton again. He was so incensed with John after he smacked him down, let alone removing his key witness. Carboni saw this as a personal affront as if John was intentionally conspiring against him, hence the reason he did not mention his name in his book. Instead he classified him in the same category as a government spy.

The Clerk of the Court didn't take Dr Carr seriously being covered in urine and alcohol. He appeared to be a street drunkard and merely told Dr Carr to fill out a form.

Dr Carr ranted and raved at the Clerk of the Court regarding his attitude. This only resulted in Dr Carr being escorted from the building, while kicking and screaming of course.

He headed off to Heaton Chapel to see his family and have it out. He arrived at the home at 6 Peel Terrace on Wednesday evening, 8th August 1855.

The housekeeper of My Mary Carr answered the door. Harriet Wier was her name. Dr Carr ranted and raved again, demanding to see his mother and brother. Harriet allowed Dr Carr to come in and clean himself up before talking with his mother.

Dalton's Gold
By Peter D Matthews

    Mary was so happy to see her son, but she was troubled by his frenzied rage. He was almost like an overheated pressure cooker, waiting to blow. She had heard from Frederick's wife, regarding his loss of mind, which was confirmed by him running off at the dock.

    Unfortunately, his brother Frederick Carr was not there that night, as he gone to Derby. Frederick's wife had arrived home but immediately went out to dine with friends. That left Mary Carr and Harriet Wier on their own that night. It was obvious that Frederick's wife didn't want to be around when Dr Carr turned up.

    Mary asked Harriet to stay close as she feared some sort of reprisal. There was a heated exchange between Dr Carr and his mother over the trickery, which moved quickly into his inheritance. Mary gave Dr Carr a silver plate as his share in the inheritance from his father. The plate was not only valuable, but was a family heirloom passed down for two generations.

    Harriet Wier observed the entire incident, as Mary requested she stay as a witness. By this time Mary was extremely upset and 'put out about it', so Harriet confirmed.

    Dr Carr came back the next night and sat at the table drinking a cup of tea, while Mary ate her supper. She sat their trembling in fear, expecting Dr Carr would start all over again. Dr Carr was relatively sedate. He served his mother a little toddy of brandy and water after her meal.

    Mary went to her quite place of solitude after dinner - her garden - for a stroll. There was no heated exchange, no major incident as the night before, but Mary was still overwhelmed with him just being there. She was concerned that he could fire up at any moment.

It was about 9:00pm on Thursday 9th August 1855, when Mary started to feel faint and called out to Dr Carr for help. Within an hour, she had a seizure and vomited, before passing away at 1:30am on 10th August 1855.

Dr Carr gave the Coroner a letter stating:

I hereby certify that I was in medical attendance upon the late Mary W Carr, of Heaton Chapel, from 09:00 pm on Aug 9th, 1855, to 1:30 am on Aug 10th, 1855, at the time of her death. The symptoms of sudden sickness and then after an hour epilepsy, were such as would be produced by a narcotic poison, such as brucine or strychnine, acting on the cerebral spinal system. I have no hesitation in giving an opinion that Mary Carr did not die of natural causes, but to the best of my belief, she was poisoned. (Signed) Alfred Yates Carr, M.D., Post Office, Stockport, 12 pm August 10th, 1855.[12]

Dr Carr accused the wife of his brother of poisoning Mary Carr and trying to blame it on him.

Harriet Wier's statement to Police confirmed that Dr Carr gave Mary Carr a glass of brandy and water before her collapse, accusing Dr Carr of poisoning Mary Carr himself.

Dalton's Gold
By Peter D Matthews

The Manchester Coroner requested an inquest into her death. Dr William Rainer performed the autopsy and provided the below report:

William Rainer, of Heaton Norris deposed :-I am a physician. I examined the body of Mary Carr last night. There were no marks of personal injury on the exterior of the body; on opening the skull and examining the brain, I found the left of the cerebellum was ruptured. The cerebellum is that portion of the brain situated behind the ear. It contained about two ounces of coagulated blood; that was the cause of death; in fact death was caused by apoplexy (stroke) affecting that portion of the brain, accompanied by the rupture of the blood vessel. The heart was considerably enlarged (hypertrophic cardiomyopathy), and any excitement would be more likely to produce such a casualty than if the heart was not in that state. The stomach and bowels presented nothing unusual, in fact they were rather in a healthy state. The stomach contained a little coffee coloured secretion. I did not analyse it because I was satisfied the cause of death was in the brain. The immediate casualty may have been caused by excitement (stress). The epileptic convulsion (seizure) was likely to be caused by the rupture of the blood vessel, more so than if it had occurred in the portion of the brain called the cerebrum, which was more the seat of the sensations. The vomiting would come on the rupture occurring, as in that state the stomach very frequently rejects its contents. After the effusion the sensibility would be a gradually annihilated, and the vomiting would cease. I know of no poison which would cause death in the same way. There was not the slightest reason for supposing that any poison had in any way caused the death; in such a system as Mrs Carr's would be, any violent emotion of the mind acting upon and increasing the power of the heart, might thereby cause the rupture of the vessels on the brain.[13] (brackets mine)

In actual fact, Dr Carr may have been right. History tells us that Strychnine has been used for many murders. The symptoms of using such a poison are: nausea, vomiting, convulsions, dilated pupils, and death usually results due to asphyxia. However stroke is also caused through a lack of oxygen supply to the brain with much the same symptoms along with weakness, numbness, and the loss of function of one side or parts of the body.

Cardiac arrest and stroke are quite normal causes of death in patients with hypertrophic cardiomyopathy. Therefore Mary Carr's death could have been caused through poison or undue stress. In actual fact it could have been Dr Carr, but it could also have been the daughter-in-law. It is possible that the housekeeper did it, and decided to take advantage of the timing with Dr Carr arriving home.

Dr Carr was so sure that his family had poisoned his mother. But then again he had just spent many months being shackled inside the belly of ship, while his sister-in-law walked around the deck free. Did he do it intentionally in the hope of pinning the murder on his sister-in-law?

Dr Carr turned to the only thing he knew to relieve his pain and anguish - the bottle. He went out on the town and while he was three parts full, he visited the Manchester Exchange and read a proclamation denouncing his family as being guilty of murder and the coroner of the county as guilty of high treason.

While he was at his mother's home, he took two pistols that belonged to his father, along with caps, balls and a bag of powder.

The following night after his proclamation at the Manchester Exchange, Dr Carr was arrested on Wednesday 15th August 1885 after another drunken rampage. He was believed to be found by Police, wandering the city streets of Manchester with his father's two pistols in his hands.

He was described by the Magistrate of New Bailey, Mt Trafford, as a 'dangerous lunatic'. On the 17th August 1855, Dr Carr was committed to Prestwich Asylum in Manchester.

John only became aware after reading a newspaper of 23rd November 1855 which read:

> Yesterday, Thursday morning, Mr Alfred Yates Carr, of Manchester was brought before Mr Trafford, magistrate of the New Bailey as a dangerous lunatic, having been found wandering about in the night with a couple of loaded pistols in his hands He had gone upon the Manchester Exchange

the evening previously also, and read a proclamation denouncing a near relative of his as guilty of murder, and the coroner of the county as guilty of high treason. Mr Carr is the same gentleman who a few days ago applied to the magistrate at Liverpool for a warrant against the captain of the James Baines, emigrant ship, for putting him in chains on his home ward voyage from Australia. Mr Trafford committed him to Prestwick Asylum as a dangerous lunatic - (reprinted from) Liverpool Mail, 18th August.[14]

John then heard the full story from other English newspapers and remaining family members. He was somehow relieved but yet gutted at the same time. Had he not sent him off to England in shackles, this would never have occurred. But at the same time John thought this may be a good thing, because he would never see Dr Carr again. Or so he thought!

The Dreaded Return of Dr Carr
Mrs Carr, wife of Dr Carr, stayed on the goldfields waiting to hear news of her husband. She had believed that Dr Carr returned to England with his sister-in-law to see the family.
In late 1856 she received a letter from Dr Carr, confirming that he was entrapped by John Dalton and taken to England. Whilst there he visited his mother

who died in his arms, after being poisoned by his sister-in-law. He was declared insane and spent the last fifteen months in an asylum. Dr Carr had escaped and was travelling back to Ballarat.

Margaret Dalton, John's wife, was furious when she heard what John had done to her uncle. Although she renounced him as her uncle, she certainly didn't expect John to do something like that.

Dr Carr alighted a ship in Melbourne on a stinking hot day and without even thinking, he belted a Mr Ellis on the way past. Mr Ellis expected an apology, but instead was given a tongue lashing for being in the way.

Believing that Dr Carr was a raving lunatic, he had Dr Carr arrested for disorderly conduct on 8th February 1857 in Melbourne.

Dr Carr didn't help his own cause as he shouted furiously in the gaol all night. When Constable Marks attended, he knocked him to the ground, so his actions confirmed the allegations by Mr Ellis.

The surgeon at the Eastern Goal, Dr Henry Scope, knew Dr Carr as he was also a member of the College of Surgeons. He remanded Dr Carr for assessment as he believed Dr Carr to be suffering from a psychiatric disorder called, 'delirium tremens'.[15]

On Wednesday 18th February 1857, Dr Carr appeared in the City Court after being charged with lunacy.

Dr Carr was given an attorney by the name of Beattie. Dr Carr protested that the fellow who was to represent him was in fact, Adam Loftus Lynn, a solicitor who had it in for him from Ballarat.

In fact he was correct, as Lynn was hired by George Scobie to discredit Dr Carr after the death of James Scobie. Dr Carr demanded to represent himself.

For Dr Carr, a Mr Vaughan appeared. He asserted that there was nothing for the Bench to remand the prisoner upon. There was merely the evidence of the surgeon of the gaol who was of opinion that he was suffering from delirum tremens which could have been caused by a drug.

He complained that Dr Carr had been very harshly treated, having been dragged through the streets of Melbourne handcuffed, which was completely unnecessary.

Dr Scope for the prosecution insisted the reason for the handcuffs was that Dr Carr tried resist arrest.

Dr M'Crae testified that the first time he saw Dr Carr, he was in a state of, 'great excitement and manifestly insane'. Dr M'Crae also affirmed that 'Dr Carr struck Dr O'Reilly. He contemplated giving him a certificate of insanity as he believed he was a risk to the public.'[16]

Dr Carr insisted that he had been drugged with coculus indicus or Indian hemp.

The Mayor of Melbourne witnessed the incident and testified that Dr Carr was, 'Unquestionably an insane man and in a state of mind from which violence might be apprehended. I considered him, in fact, to be a dangerous lunatic - there was not the least question about it.'[17]

Dr O'Reilly was next to testify. He stated that he had known Dr Carr from childhood, that they went to school together. He had lived in Dr Carr's house and was a friend of the family.

He testified that Dr Carr may have seemed to be insane by his behaviour, and confirmed Dr Carr did strike him but believed the whole ordeal aboard the James Baines had caused Dr Carr to act in this way. He believed he was still a competent surgeon.

Dr O'Reilly believed the gaolers actions of refusing to allow him to post a letter to his wife, then handcuffing him was the wrong thing to do, based upon his previous experience being shackled in the bowels of a ship for months.

His friend, the captain of the ship Persia, was prepared to take him on board the ship as the ship's surgeon, rather than sending him to an asylum.

The magistrate freed Dr Carr to the Persia but on the basis he must reside on the ship.

There are no further records to confirm what happened in the next twenty-four hours, nor were family aware of what happened, but the next day Dr Carr was arrested on shore for some reason, and was committed to the Yarra Bend Lunatic Asylum for the rest of his natural life.

In 1859 Dr Carr submitted a scathing report at to the treatment of patients at the Asylum to the Victoria

Legislative Assembly which resulted in a Royal Commission investigation.

During that investigation many patients testified, including Dr Carr who said:

> I had been in solitary confinement for some days under restraint, wearing a strait waistcoat, fastened by a padlock. Over the waistcoat there was a bag, open at the bottom, and with long sleeves, by tying behind great pain could be caused by the attendants if they chose. These bags were left me for seven or eight days.[18]

However Dr Carr repeatedly escaped from the asylum in Melbourne. Each time he was arrested trying to get back to Ballarat. Headlines regularly featured Dr Carr's escape. He was described as, 'The most dangerous man in the asylum'.

The Legislative Assembly learned that Dr Carr was owed £126 and also 1,000 guineas for medical services rendered at Ballarat in providing medical attention to the injured officers after the attack. This was while he was in the government camp. Eventually he was awarded £150 compensation.

In 1887, he was moved to the Ararat Asylum, some 87 km west of Smythesdale to be closer to the family. He passed away on 26 June 1894 in his sleep. A Coroner determined the following day that Dr Carr died of hypertrophic cardiomyopathy, which was the exact same heart disease that his mother died of. He was 78 years of age.

Constable J.T. McCuskey of the Ararat Police had his body buried in the Ararat Cemetery on 28 June 1894 and family were not informed. John and Margaret Dalton were only informed by the asylum when they visited months later. One can only imagine how John felt as he learned of Dr Carr's death.

11
STATE TRIALS

One by one, each prisoner was shackled and dragged from the gaol to the adjacent building for the trial. In 1855 the Supreme Court of Melbourne was an obtrusive three storey bluestone building on the corner of La Trobe Terrace and Russell Street. It manifested itself as a place of disgust and dread to the prisoners.

The three arches to the front of the building could easily have had ropes hanging down from each arch, for each of the three judges to hang their victims from.

To the side of the old stone courthouse was two relatively new timber courtrooms which were equally obtrusive and feared. Next to this was the old Melbourne Gaol, where the prisoners were held in deplorable conditions. They were given nothing more than a board and a blanket to sleep on a cold damp slate floor. Those in remand were crammed like animals into dark, dismal, mind numbing cells.

The conditions were so reprehensible that many men would rather take their own lives, than be confined in such debased conditions. They waited in despair to hear of their mates that went before them, only to return from the court, to be hung on the gallows and buried in an unmarked grave without a head.

The screaming, shrieking and sobbing at night would send any sane man senseless. For this the gaoler had a special treatment - an iron mask and thick leather gloves, supposedly to stop the prisoner harming themselves.

Amongst those in the prison were men, women and even children; from lunatics, to vagrants, to some of the most notorious hardened criminals - murderers, rapists, robbers and even those accused of treason.

The food, if you can call it that, was a watery swill of dried maize with half a dozen grains of rice and the odd weevil or grub for added protein of course. If they were fortunate enough, every so often they would receive a slice of old sour mouldy bread to soak up the swill.

Solitary confinement prevented any outside contact with the real world. They were released for exercise one hour a day, where they could not even speak to other prisoners. This was zealously enforced using a silence mask or a calico hood which had two holes for the eyes only. The prisoners dare not communicate. For good behaviour the prisoners were taken higher up the prison where they had certain privileges - like communicating with one another!

This also had its downfalls though. Four or five men were crammed tight into a cell of twelve feet by three feet but still with nothing more than a blanket and a board.

Bathing and changing clothes was a necessity they were denied but once a week. Chapel came on Sunday where the priest would visit the prison for an hour and a half. That is, unless something else came up, which quiet often did.

But what angered the prisoners more than anything was the fully naked searches of every orifice once a week. It seemed the debauched prison guards took great delight in this reprehensible activity. The conditions in the prison were deplorable and frankly intolerable, to say the least.

On 23rd January 1855 the thirteen diggers of Ballarat arrived at the Old Melbourne Gaol. It was 8:00pm and almost dark. Governor Hotham was waiting to personally eye ball the prisoners who were accused of rebelling against the Queen.

Hotham wore a three piece dark suit with white fine linen high collared shirt, which was finished with an audacious cravat. He was a striking sight to the filthy diggers who were covered in a thick coat of dust from the long tiresome trip from Ballarat.

Hotham inspected the diggers, before they were strip searched and secured away in solitary confinement for six days. They were not let out until they were to appear in court to enter a plea.

On 29 January 1855, six days after their arrival in Melbourne, the thirteen diggers of Ballarat faced the bench to enter their plea before the staunch Chief Justice, Sir William a'Beckett.

As first Chief Justice to the Supreme Court of Victoria, he was highly critical of the effects the goldfields had upon the colony. He released a guide for Magistrates titled, 'Does the Discovery of Gold in Victoria, viewed in relation to its Moral and Social Effects as hitherto developed, deserve to be considered a National Blessing or a National Curse'.

Sir William a'Beckett believed the gold rush was a national curse upon the good society of Australia. He saw the thirteen diggers that stood before him as the scourge of the land. a'Beckett was extremely self opinionated and easily agitated.

That is why Hotham insisted that His Honour, Chief Justice, Sir William a'Beckett preside over the first two scheduled trials. This was to ensure a conviction of the ringleaders, Timothy Hayes and Raffaello Carboni.

Timothy Hayes was first to enter his plea but he hesitated. He seemed to be arguing with his counsel. The other twelve ended up standing before the bench to enter their plea of 'not guilty'. Timothy Hayes' counsel tried to convince him to do the same.

Hayes' mind was suffering with what we would now call Post Traumatic Stress Disorder from seeing his mates massacred before his own eyes by the government. That was hard enough but to be arrested and dragged to Melbourne with the distinct possibility of being hung, was too much to bear. Life had been turned upside down. It was no wonder that he struggled to enter a plea.

He had just spent the past six days in solitary confinement and was dragged before a judge who was clearly predisposed to hanging him.

'Would it not be easier to plead guilty and be hanged quickly, than to plead not guilty and go through a whole lot more pain and suffering, only to be hanged anyway' he thought.

His barrister assured him it was worth waiting and defending the charges, asserting that he should plead 'not guilty' like the others.

Later that day, Timothy Hayes also pleaded, 'not guilty' before the Supreme Court. His counsel managed to convince him that if he pleaded guilty, his mates would also been seen as being guilty.

All the diggers were remanded in custody for trial proceedings to start on 22nd February 1855.

After what happened at Ballarat, Hotham didn't seem to learn his lesson from this massacre of Australian diggers. He reordered licence hunts in Bendigo and Castlemaine, which resulted in the burning of their licences too. Yet he pressed on against the thirteen charged with high treason, despite enormous public outcry.

Clearly the government wanted to delay the trials to wear down the prisoners in gaol. So violated by the deplorable conditions, the diggers wrote to the Sheriff of the Colony of Victoria, pleading for clemency:

Dalton's Gold
By Peter D Matthews

SIR – As the chief officer of the Government regulating Prison Discipline in Victoria, we, the undersigned Ballarat state prisoners, respectfully beg to acquaint you with the mode of our treatment since our imprisonment in this Gaol, in the hope that you will have the goodness to make some alterations for the better.

At seven o'clock in the morning we are led into a small yard of about thirty yards long and eight wide where we must either stand, walk or sent (print not readable) upon the cold earth (no seats or benches were afforded us), and which at meal times serves chair, table, &c., with the additional consequence of having our food saturated with sand (print not readable) and with every kind of disgusting filth which the wind may happen to stir up within the yard.

We are locked in about three o'clock in the afternoon, four or five of us together, in a cell whose dimensions are three feet by twelve, being thus debarred from the free air of heaven for sixteen hours out of the twenty-four. The food is of the very worst description ever used by civilised beings. We are debarred the use of writing materials except for purposes of pressing necessity; are never permitted to see a newspaper; and strictly prohibited the use of tobacco and snuff; we have been subjected to the annoyance of being sometimes stripped naked, a dozen men together, when a process of 'searching' takes place which is debasing to any human being, but perfectly revolting to men whose sensibilities have never been blunted by familiarity with crime – an ordeal of examination, and the coarse audacity with which it is perpetrated, as would make manhood blush, and which it would assuredly resent, as an outrage upon common decency in any other place than a prison. And again, when the visiting Justice takes his rounds, we are made to stand bareheaded before him.

We give the Government the credit of believing that it is not its wish we should be treated with such unsparing malignity and apparent malice, and also believe that, if you, Sir, the representative of Government, in this Department, had been previously been made acquainted with this mode of treatment you would have caused it to be altered. But we have hitherto refrained from troubling the Government on the subject, in expectation of a speedy trial, which now appears to be postponed sign die. We, each of us, can look back with laudable pride upon our lives, and not a page in the record of the past can unfold a single transgression which would degrade us before man, or for which, we would be condemned before our Maker.

And we naturally ask why we should be treated as if our lives had been one succession of crime, or as if society breathe freely once more at being rid of our dangerous and demoralising presence. Even the Sunday that to all men in Christendom is a day of relaxation and comparative enjoyment, is for us one of gloom and weariness, being locked up in a dreary cell from three o'clock Saturday evening, til seven on Sunday morning (except for about an hour and a half on Sunday), thus locked up in a narrow dungeon for forty consecutive hours, we appeal to you, and ask was there ever worse treatment in the worst days of the Roman Inquisition, for men whose reputation had never been sullied with crime?

We therefore humbly submit that, as the State only looks at present to our being well secured we ought to be treated with every liberality consistent with our safe

custody, and that any unnecessary harshness or arrogant display of power, is nothing more or less than wanton cruelty. Some of us for instance, could while away several hours each day in writing, an occupation which, while it would fill up the dreary vacuum of a prison life, would lend elasticity to the mind, as would the moderate use of snuff and tobacco, cheer it and soothe that mental irritation consequent upon seclusion. But that system of discipline which would paralyse the mind and debilitate the body – that would
destroy intellectual as well as physical energy and vigor, cannot certainly be of human origin.
Trusting you will remove these sources of annoyance and complaint,
We beg to subscribe ourselves,
Sir Your obedient servants,
Here follows the names.[19]

The above letter was published in The Age newspaper in Melbourne on 14th February 1855. This angered the general population throughout Australia. The media helped this by publishing scathing attacks in almost every newspaper nationwide.

John Dalton read this report in the newspaper and his heart sunk so deep. He was distraught for his mates but what would happen if he went to Melbourne? This was his mates that he sat around the fire with, now locked up in a cramped cell under extreme duress in appalling conditions. Should he speak up and risk his own life? He thought, 'These brutes will not listen to me. They'll just lock me up too. But I must go the trials. I can't turn my back on my mates.'

Timothy Hayes trial was the first to be heard on 22nd February 1855, then Carboni. Because Dr Carr couldn't be found as a witness and John Manning's barrister was supposedly ill, the trial of John Joseph was first.

This was a strategic act by the Prosecutor, the Attorney-General himself, Sir William Foster Stawell. He was a close friend and personal advisor to Governor Hotham. Many believed he was the one in Hotham's ear who was driving the stern determination. Stawell was adamantly opposed to the export duty on gold which was proposed by the diggers.

John Joseph was selected by the Crown as he was an uneducated African American digger who was abandoned by his own countrymen. The Americans left him to rot in an Australian gaol, only to be hanged, simply because of his colour.

The Prosecutor saw Joseph as an easy conviction. He was easily identified by the witnesses, and after all, no jury would have any reservedness in convicting a 'riotous nigger'. This idiom became the catchphrase of the day.

To the Crown, this trial was of significant importance, as John Joseph was accused of firing the first shot that killed Captain Wise.

John Dalton knew this was not true as the government had fired first shot and the Independent Californian Rangers returned fire only after Lalor realized that it was 'defend of die'. It was certainly not John Joseph who shot Captain Wise - it was an Independent Californian Ranger.

John Joseph was an armed digger at the time of the attack. He had not long moved to the diggings but yet stood side-by-side defending his new found mates. He wielded a double barrel shotgun with only two rounds of ammo. When that ran out, he picked up a pike. Joseph fought valiantly before being arrested by Sub-Inspector Charles Carter. John Dalton was proud to stand and call John Joseph an Aussie mate.

The thirteen diggers about to be tried for high treason, stood before a hanging judge and a hostile prosecutor, both intent on hanging each of the diggers. What chance did these diggers have?

The answer is simple - their right under the Magna Carta of 1215, which gave them the right to a fair trial by a jury of twelve peers of the community. Without this right, the diggers were destined to hang on the Melbourne gallows.

The Queen v John Joseph

The bright demeanour of John Joseph surprised the crowd as he was brought into the Supreme Court in chains on 22nd February 1855. Less a man would at least have had a scowl upon their face, but no, not John Joseph, who was aptly nicknamed "Uncle Tom". He wore a fearless beam which lit up his face.

    It was not so much his dark skin that set him apart to the diggers on the goldfields. Nor was it his long black sideburns that came down almost to his shaven chin. But it was his bright demeanour and devout Christian principles that that picked him out in the crowd. He was a gentle kind-hearted person, always smiling, even on the most dull day. He was willing to do anything for a mate. That is what set him apart.

    Joseph was nicknamed 'Uncle Tom' after the 1852 bestselling book of the 19th century titled, 'Uncle Tom's Cabin' by Harriet Beecher Stowe.

    The main character of her book was 'Uncle Tom'. He was an African American slave who believed Christian love could overcome everything, including slavery, or in John Joseph's case - even his time in gaol.

    The solemn courtroom was filled beyond capacity. Some ten thousand people from all over the country turned up to hear the proceedings. People were gathered outside the courtroom to the point of filling the streets.

    The air in the courtroom was thick, filled with nervousness and uncertainty. The crowd was quite boisterous after hearing of the treatment of the diggers. Tension resinated from the prosecution as they feared the massive crowd. After all, Melbourne only had a population of one hundred thousand people and ten thousand had turned up for this monumental occasion.

Appearing for the defence of John Joseph was a young enthusiastic 25 year old barrister named Butler Cole Aspinall and twenty seven years his senior, declared 'Philosophic Radical' barrister, Henry Chapman.

The 'all rise' command came from the associate as Chief Justice William a'Beckett entered the courtroom. A sudden, almost deadly quiet came over the courtroom. None dare speak otherwise they would be held in contempt of court.

The first order of business was the selection of the jury. The Prosecutor, the Attorney-General himself, Sir William Foster Stawell acted for the Crown.

The Attorney-General in an attempt to be seen to be selective, removed anyone from the jury who looked like a labourer, digger or publican, or more to the point, anyone with an Irish accent.

Thirty jurors were challenged before being accepted by the Crown. John Joseph threw a spanner in the works objecting to gentlemen and merchants. To throw Joseph off, the government titled some as 'licensed victuallers', rather than merchants as they wanted some influence in the jury. A licensed victualler was a merchant of sorts, as they operated a business supplying victuals or food supplies to the military. The government were up to their old tricks again - these men were in fact contract suppliers to the military of this very same government.

The uneducated John Joseph did not realize the definition, but one would think that his team of barristers would have picked this up. As they were not being paid by John Joseph but by the court, it was clear who they were really working for.

The list of jury members are listed below, noting no Irish, no labourers, no diggers but two gentlemen and two licensed victuallers:

1. Sampson Wise, of George Street, a gentleman;
2. Frederick Whitmore, of Gertrude Street, a saddler;
3. James William Wood, of Gertrude Street, a victualler;
4. Edward Wills, of Hanover Street, a stone merchant;
5. Frederick Waters, of Smith Street, a butcher;
6. William Watts, of Wreckyn Street, a carpenter;
7. James Westwood, of Napier Street, a gentleman;
8. Jacob Wood, of Smith Street, a victualler;
9. William Wallace, of Victoria Street, a householder;
10. James Wyllie, of Little Howard Street, a householder;
11. Henry K. Woodsworth, of Howard Street, a coffee roaster;
12. James Wilson, of Great Brighton, a bookseller.[20]

Dalton's Gold
By Peter D Matthews

The jury were sworn in and the charges were read again to the court in front of the jury:

John Joseph, the charge against you in the first count is, that you did, on the 3rd December, 1854, being at the time armed in a warlike manner, traitorously assemble together against our Lady the Queen; and that you did, whilst so armed and assembled together, levy and make war against our said Lady the Queen, within that part of her dominions called Victoria, and attempt by force of arms to destroy the Government constituted there and by law established, and to depose our Lady the Queen from the kingly name and her Imperial Crown.

In the second count you are charged with having made war, as in the first count mentioned, and with attempting at the same time to compel by force our said Lady the Queen to change her measures and counsels.

In the third count the charge against you is, that having devised and intended to deprive our said Lady the Queen of the kingly name of the Imperial Crown in Victoria, you did express and evince such treasonable intention by the four following overt acts:

That you raised upon a pole, and collected round a certain standard, and did solemnly swear to defend each other, with the intention of levying war against our said Lady the Queen.

That being armed with divers offensive weapons, you collected together and formed troops and bands under distinct leaders, and were drilled and trained in military exercise, to prepare for fighting against the soldiers and other loyal subjects of the Queen.

That you collected and provided arms and ammunition, and erected divers fences and stockades, in order to levy war against our said Lady the Queen.

That being armed and arrayed in a warlike manner, you fired upon. fought with, wounded, and killed divers of the said soldiers and other subjects then fighting in behalf of our said Lady the Queen, contrary to duty and allegiance.

In the fourth count the charge against you is, that having devised and levy war against the Queen, in order to compel her by force and constraint her measures and counsels, you did express and evince such treasonable and divers acts, which overt acts are four in number, and the same as those described in the third count.[21]

Dalton's Gold
By Peter D Matthews

The government believed it was an open and shut case for John Joseph due to his distinctive appearance. They had statements from twelve so-called witnesses including one of the diggers. They were: Henry Goodenough - a Government spy who was actually a Trooper; Andrew Peters - Trooper; Daniel Haggerty - Sergeant of 40th Regiment; Charles Carter - Sub-Inspector of Police; Patrick O'Keefe - Private; John Donnelly - Private; James Harris - Sergeant of 40th Regiment; Gilbert Andrew Amos - Commissioner; Charles Prendergast Hackett Esq. - Police magistrate; George Webster - Government spy who was actually a Police Magistrate; Thomas Allen - Storekeeper at Eureka and former red-toad from the 33rd Regiment; and Raffaello Carboni of all people who appeared against a fellow digger.[22]

The jury listened to the witnesses who were mostly government employees or spies. The prosecutor though had an uphill battle because he had to prove 'beyond reasonable doubt' that John Joseph had 'treasonable intent' against the Queen and her servants.

The Attorney-General argued, 'if men were allowed to organize such a conspiracy as this, there is no saying how many wrongheaded men, acting with zeal – but misguided zeal – might be led into the commission of the most dreadful crimes and outrages.'[23]

Asserting that he was a conspirator was one thing but proving it was a completely different story. The government had to prove that John Joseph actively participated in war against the Queen in attempting to overthrow her government. He also had to prove that Joseph attempted to kill representatives of the Queen in an act to overthrow the government to enable a conviction of high treason. This was going to be tall order.

The barristers for his defence, picking up on his Ballarat nickname Uncle Tom, they asserted that Joseph may have been a 'riotous nigger' but more likely an 'Uncle Tom', and as such a person of that character clearly would not have had 'treasonable intent' against the Queen.

John and a number of other witnesses volunteered to testify in favour of the diggers.

'Involving a number of witnesses would only complicate matters' John was told by Henry Chapman, barrister for John Joseph.

John couldn't help thinking, 'Are they acting for John Joseph or the prosecution?'

John could insist all he like but at the end of the day, he was not in charge of the defence - the barristers were.

Rather than bring in John Dalton who offered to provide evidence at the trial for the defence, they opted to have no witnesses appear and let the jury decide.

The defence wanted a clean cut undisputable verdict of not guilty, based upon the evidence presented by the government. Or was it they were instructed not to call any witnesses in the hope that the jury would convict him?

The jury retired to carefully examine the evidence and within half an hour they emerged with a decision.

The verdict of 'not guilty' was read in the courtroom and the crowd erupted with shouts of jubilation which bellowed into the streets.

The incensed Chief Justice a'Beckett saw this as an attempt by the general public to influence the jury in the following trials. He was outraged and demanded silence in his court room.

The Attorney-General pointed out two men in the crowd that had loudly applauded and seemed to have stirred up the crowd. Chief Justice a'Beckett sentenced these two men, John Keogh and George Gordon, to a week in prison for contempt of court.

Typical of the Australian government - they sought to push the charges up to the highest possible, which became their own downfall.

Instead of charging them with 'affray' or 'riot' which would have had them convicted, Hotham chose to push the charges up to 'high treason', which most certainly could not be proved that John Joseph had such 'treasonable intent' against the Queen.

To the ordinary citizens of the jury, also disillusioned with Hotham's government, this was nonsense.

The diggers were merely protecting themselves from being slaughtered while protesting against the government for their exorbitant taxes and the brutal method they used in collecting it.

Dalton's Gold
By Peter D Matthews

John Joseph was an honest, upright and well liked Aussie digger. This illiterate man was no exciter of the people. Nor had he any political motivation to perpetrate war against the Crown. He was merely protecting himself and his mates from being slaughtered like animals.

The jury had no choice but acquit him.

On being discharged from the court, John Joseph had his mind set on returning to Ballarat, but the ecstatic crowd had other ideas. He was surrounded with cheering and shouting and a chair came through the crowd for him to be seated. So excited was the crowd that they carried him upon their shoulders around the city streets of Melbourne. This was a triumph not only for John Joseph but for every Australian.

While the crowd applauded, the Attorney-General cringed. He looked over his next case carefully in the hope that the two men for contempt would subdue the crowd before the next trial.

The Queen v John Manning

The trial of John Manning really concerned John Dalton. He knew John Manning was a Captain and Council Member of the Ballarat Reform League.

Manning was not a gold digger but a school teacher at St Alipius Catholic School as well as part time reporter for Henry Seekamp at the Ballarat Times.

Seekamp was arrested after the Eureka bloodbath for seditious libel against the government. The government blamed him as the publisher for printing treasonable statements such as this excerpt of 18 November 1854, which was read by John Dalton during his honeymoon:

> No power on earth can now restrain the united might and headlong strides for freedom of the people of this country...The League has undertaken a mighty task fit only for a great people - that of changing the dynasty of the country.[24]

Although Seekamp was the publisher of the newspaper, everyone knew it was John Manning that was the author these seditious reports against the government.

Seekamp was convicted on 25th January 1855, and spent time in the same gaol as the diggers. The jury insisted on mercy as the authorship of these articles was proven not to be Seekamp himself, but those in his employ. The government again played a strategic game and held back his sentencing hearing until after the state trials.

John Manning was in the stockade during the attack. He was found by Sub-Inspector Carter hiding in a tent. Manning was handed over to the 40th regiment and was marched off to the government camp, before the troopers went wild killing the wounded and burning everything to the ground.

Although the government knew that Manning wrote these seditious articles in the newspaper, they couldn't prove it. Seekamp was loyal to his employees, unfortunately to his own detriment.

The evidence against Manning was circumstantial at best. Melbourne newspapers closely monitored the cases of Henry Seekamp and John Manning. The Australian media were already critical of the government but had to carefully scrutinize the government's hard stance to ensure they too were not arrested.

The trial of John Manning commenced on Monday 26th February 1855. As Manning was taken from the gaol there were shouts of 'not guilty' throughout the massive crowd, who gathered to protest against the government's treatment of the diggers.

Again Chief Justice a'Beckett presided over the matter, along with the Attorney-General, Sir William Stawell, as Prosecutor.

Manning's solicitor was Scottish born James Grant who was a well respected solicitor of Melbourne. He had significant legal experience in media matters. Counsel for his defence was none other than Archibald Michie, an associate (Junior Barrister) to Thomas a'Beckett who was the brother to the presiding Chief Justice. It was abundantly clear to John Dalton and all of his fellow diggers, why Michie had offered his services for free.

Fortunately for Manning, Michie was assisted by Senior Counsel Joseph Dunne, who was a local Ballarat barrister. John Dalton was friends with Joseph Dunne. He had stayed regularly at the Bath Hotel during the time John and Margaret stayed there. John had dinner and drinks with him on a number of occasions. They talked of the good old days in Ireland which was interesting to John as his family were from Ireland but he had never been to Ireland himself. But of course he did not let on in front of Margaret.

James Grant signalled Manning during jury selection, asking Manning to strike off any juror that he indicated. The jury selection took longer than the actual trial and both the Crown and the defence rejected many jurors.

The final Jury consisted of twelve local people of Melbourne but the trial records did not confirm where they were from. They merely recorded their names without address or occupation. They were:

Henry Williamson;
Thomas Ward;
John W. Waugh;
Alfred Watson;
Frederick Walters;
James Wise;
James Watkin;
John Walker;
George Walker;
Edward Young;
Henry Young;
David Watt.[25]

The government paraded much the same witnesses including Henry Goodenough, Andrew Peters,

George Webster, Charles Hackett, George Amos, Charles Carter with the addition of the following people:
>William Dalgleish - a Trooper;
>Michael Quigley - an undercover Spy who was a Trooper;
>John King - a Police Inspector who seized the Southern Cross flag;
>Thomas Mills who we know little about;
>John Dougherty - a Trooper who previously gave false evidence regarding the burning of Eureka Hotel;
>Thomas Allen - the Proprietor of Waterloo Coffee House who formerly served in the 33rd Regiment.

Manning's legal team, apart from Michie, were resolute on an acquittal. There was a distinct lack of evidence against John Manning presented by the government. The major impediment to the Attorney-General's case was the inconsistencies between Henry Goodenough's and Andrew Peters' statements regarding the number of people at the meeting at Bakery Hill. This was even questioned by a juror during summing up.[26]

Chief Justice a'Beckett in summation almost retracted his opening statement of being unbiased and having no interest in the result of their deliberations. He remarked in response to the jurors query, 'Few ever agree to the numbers'.

Any judge would normally question the validity of witness testimonies if there was any discrepancy. It was clear to all in the courtroom that Chief Justice a'Beckett was in fact considerably biased in the outcome of the trials.

Within a half an hour the jury returned with a verdict of 'not guilty'.

After the gaoling of Keogh and Gordon, the crowd although jubilant, subdued their emotions until they left the courtroom. John Manning headed off from the court room running with his mates, in the hope that he wasn't caught up in the crowd.

The government were reeling. Two of the thirteen were freed. This sent a shiver up the spine of the Attorney-General.

John Dalton would have loved to have been a fly on the wall to hear the conversation between the Attorney-General and Hotham after the trial. Hotham was no doubt offended and distraught over the acquittals.

Delay Tactics

Sir William Stawell requested the court grant a month's stay of execution on the further trials of the diggers who were held in custody, to enable the prosecutors to review the charges.

Fearful of all the diggers being acquitted by the jury and making a mockery of the government, the prosecutor was forced to do something. But what sinister scheme had he afoot? Only time would tell.

Dalton's Gold
By Peter D Matthews

Hotham in his report to his superiors after the first two trials, by his own admission in the below letter he implicates himself directly in the dastardly scheme:

> Despatch No. 38
> Reporting the result of the trial of two of the Ballarat rioters, at the Supreme Court Toorak – near Melbourne 28th February 1855
> The Right Honourable Sir George Grey Bart, K.C.B.
> Sir,
> I have already done myself the honour to report, in my Despatch No.162 of the 20th day of December 1854, that the Military force engaged in the attack on the 'Eureka' Stockade on the Gold Field at Ballarat had made one hundred and twenty prisoners; out of this number only thirteen were committed for trial; the remainder being released, not on account of the charges being entirely disproved, but because the Magistrates were to limit the commitments to those against whom the proof of participation was of the clearest kind.
> The prisoners already named were sent to Melbourne to take their trial; but for various causes, into which I need hardly enter, the trials were postponed until the

Dalton's Gold
By Peter D Matthews

20th day of February when, at the request of the Counsel of the first three prisoners their trial was further postponed, in consequence of the alleged absence of material witnesses for the Defence of the first two, and the want of preparation on the part of the third to take his trial.

The case of the fourth, a person of colour, and an inhabitant of Boston in the United States, was then proceeded with.

I append for your information a copy of the report of the trial extracted from the 'Argus' newspaper, and a complete report of these trials – taken from a short hand writers notes, will be transmitted as soon as they can be prepared.

The Identity of the prisoner – his presence on two occasions when the insurgents were being armed and drilled, and his presence at and participation in, the occurrences at the Eureka Stockade on the morning of the 3rd December, were clearly proved.

Six witnesses spoke to his having been found inside the stockade – two to his having been seen discharging a gun at the Military – and two to his having been taken in custody, out of a tent inside the Stockade, which was used as a Guard Tent by the Insurgents, and from which many shots had been fired – many persons having been found dead and wounded in it, and several stand of arms having been discovered lying on the floor apparently recently discharged.

The proof of existence of a treasonable concert, was supported by evidence of the meeting on Bakery Hill on the 28th of November – the swearing in of volunteers under the Insurgents Flag on the 29th – and the drilling of armed bodies of men on that, and the subsequent days – the compulsory stopping, by the Insurgents in armed parties, of all mining operations by the well disposed, during those days – the collection of arms, ammunition, provisions, and stores without payment – the formation of weapons (pikes) – the construction of the stockade, and the resistance and attack (the firing having been commenced by the Insurgents without challenge or parley) on the troops, and constabulary, on the morning of the 3rd December.

No evidence was called for the defence – the prisoner's Counsel resting solely on the non-existence, as they alleged, of any treasonable intentions – and the Jury, after a brief consultation of half an hour, returned a verdict of 'not guilty'.

Dalton's Gold
By Peter D Matthews

The trial of the third prisoner, Irishman, who had been, at the time of the riots, employed as a Reporter of a Newspaper published at the Goldfields – 'The Ballarat Times' – was the next.

The evidence for the prosecution in his early case, was substantially the same as that in the case of Joseph – except that there was no proof of his having been seen with arms when inside the stockade, or of having been armed when he was taken from the Guard Tent with Joseph – it was proved that he had been drilled on the previous days in the use of a pike.

No evidence was addressed for his defence – which was the same as that urged for Joseph – and a similar verdict of acquittal was, after a brief deliberation, also given in his case.

After these verdicts had been returned it was considered expedient to postpone the trial of the other prisoners until the next session, in order that in cases of such importance to the Country, the opinion of a Jury taken from another panel, might be obtained as to the guilt, or innocence, of the accused.

I have the honour to be Sir, Your most obedient humble servant.

Chas. Hotham[27] (underline mine)

Dalton's Gold
By Peter D Matthews

Everyone knew Hotham and his cohorts intentionally protracted the trials. After seeing the newspaper articles of the Ballarat diggers living in deplorable conditions in gaol and now their trials delayed, the Bendigo diggers wrote on 13th March 1855, cautioning the government in their 'sowing seeds of discontent' and pursing 'vengeance'. This was also published in almost every newspaper:

At a Meeting of The Committee of the Bendigo Reform League held at The Criterion Hotel, Sandhurst on the Evening of Wednesday the 7th of March it was Resolved:

That this Committee having carefully considered the circumstances attending the postponement of the State Trials are of opinion that the unprecedented course adopted by the Attorney General is most discreditable to any Government subversive of the benefits of Trial by Jury and evincing an unbecoming desire for vengeance;

And this Committee would earnestly warn the Government against the inevitable consequences of such proceedings the sowing of the seeds of discontent and disaffection among the people and periling of the Loyalty of the Colonists to the British Crown and that these are likely to be the consequences on this Gold Field this Committee records its solemn conviction.

And this Committee would urge upon the Government that the Peace of the Country and Justice to the Prisoners demands the immediate abandonment of the State Trials and the restoration of the Prisoners to Freedom.

    Robert Benson, Chairman
    Richard Baker
    James Egan Hall
    William Meaton
    Angus Mackay
    F.R J Dixon
    William D.C Denovan
    Edmund Hanrem
    R P. Ravenfield[28]

    Despite the public chorus of disapproval, the trials continued. Hotham's hard handed retribution against the diggers resulted in widespread disgruntlement. Even his once loyal supporters questioned his judgement in pursuing convictions at any cost.

    The delay allowed the Attorney-General, Sir William Stawell, time to prepare a list of 178 specially selected jurors from varied professions, that they believed could be relied upon to ensure convictions. From premeditated murder, they now turn to corrupting the courts, in order to secure a conviction against the remaining diggers.

The Queen v Timothy Hayes

    What angered John Dalton most of all was the case against Timothy Hayes, as he was not even in the stockade when the government attacked.

Hayes had told John late on the evening before the attack that he was going up to see Father Smyth at the chapel. John never saw Hayes return before the attack. After hearing the torrent of gunfire, Hayes raced back to stockade. Timothy Hayes was arrested on his way back to the stockade, some 300 metres away.

Attorney-General Stawell believed they were sure of a conviction with their selected predisposed jury.

The Judge was changed to Justice Redmond Barry who was known as 'the hanging judge'. He was renowned for his illogically harsh sentencing of prisoners - the same judge who later hanged Ned Kelly.

Hotham had been struck with an almighty blow with the acquittal of the diggers. 'Hang the whole lot' was the instruction from Hotham as he moved to protect his position as Governor of the colony. After all he was the one who went to 'war against the diggers'. The government pulled out all the stops and were set on a conviction.

Hayes' barrister was a brilliant but unrecognized 30 year old man by the name of Richard Ireland, who of course with a surname like that was from Ireland.

The jury was settled with no gentlemen; no spies; mainly tradespeople and farmers - none of which had an Irish accent:

1. James Bishop, of Brighton Road, a stonemason;
2. Thomas Albury, of Great Brighton, a carter;

3. Frederick Batchelder, of East Prahran, a butcher;
4. Josiah Bouchier, of Chapel Street, Prahran, a storekeeper;
5. Richard Bloxey, of Chapel Street, Prahran, a horse dealer;
6. James Brown, of Richmond Flat, a brewer;
7. Francis Bradley, of Burgundy Street, a farmer;
8. Richard Barnes, of Upper Hawthorn, a gardener;
9. Henry Beardsall, of Upper Hawthorn, a storekeeper;
10. George Bickerdyte, of Upper Hawthorn, a farmer;
11. John Blacklock, of Richmond Road, a grocer;
12. Charles W Barry, of Stone Street, a storekeeper.[29]

Ireland ruled the court room with his charming and jovial personality, yet in an instant turned the tables upon key witnesses. His harsh outburst of criticism towards the witnesses made many of them stumble into error.

Once the error was blurted from the mouth of the unsuspecting witness, Ireland quickly returned to his charming eloquence to tear their testimony to shreds. His tongue lashed like whip - cracking the atmosphere with a thunderous growl, which sent the witnesses into confusion and error.

The case against Timothy Hayes was won by Ireland's cross examination against the government spy, Henry Goodenough. He proved himself to fall far short of his name - Good enough. His testimony twisted and changed to the point of perjuring himself. He looked a complete fool to an already suspicious jury, which reflected badly upon the Attorney-General.

John Dalton was excited as he stood at the back of the courtroom, listening to the articulate exchanges. 'Ireland had Goodenough pinned down in the corner so to speak but would he lay the fatal blow?' John thought.

Henry Goodenough had asserted that Hayes at the meeting on Bakery Hill had called for men to, 'Take up arms in our defence', then during questioning, he contradicted himself repeatedly.

Ireland took the opportunity, 'Did you not swear a moment ago that nobody did say that?'

'Say, take up arms in our defence?' Goodenough asked to clarify the question.

Ireland responds with an unsettling question. He carefully declared, 'Yes. That will do. At this meeting on Wednesday was not the murder of Scobie discussed?'

The very name of James Scobie shook Goodenough to the core, wondering whether Ireland had evidence to implicate him.

'I did not hear it' stuttered Goodenough.

Ireland asks, 'Were you not examined on Bentley's trial?'

Dalton's Gold
By Peter D Matthews

John Dalton thought, 'Here we go. The truth is about to come out. Was this the final blow?'

'No' Goodenough answered in a rather sheepish tone.

'Not about the burning of the Eureka?' Ireland asks.

'No' Goodenough insists.

John was expecting Ireland to ask the question directly, 'Did you burn down the Eureka Hotel?' But no. Ireland moved on.

The cunning Ireland was not out to fry Henry Goodenough, but to discredit the government and particularly Hotham.

Out of the mouth of Goodenough before the Supreme Court, Ireland questioned him about the nature of licence hunts on the goldfields. Goodenough confirmed they were hunting men in the collection of taxes. Then Ireland turned to the regularity of the licence hunts was brought forward to once a week, instead of once a month, after Hotham's visit, to directly implicate Hotham.

The Attorney General protests, 'Does your Honour think this is evidence', not realizing where Ireland was headed.

Ireland quickly replied before the judge got the opportunity to reply, 'I wish to show the motive and I have a right to show what the conduct of the Government is'.

Turning to Goodenough on the stand, Ireland questioned, 'Was His Excellency on the diggings about that time or before?'

Goodenough confirmed, 'Some time before this'.

Justice Barry intercepted to quickly cut off the line of questioning as Justice Barry could see where he was headed. Justice Barry addresses Ireland, 'You are asking whether His Excellency was on the Goldfields; it is quite immaterial, as it seems to me.'

This opened a can of worms that the government did not want exposed.

Ireland defensively communicated, 'I think it very material to the defence of the prisoner, your Honour'.

Reeling to protect the reputation of the Governor, Justice Barry responded, 'Whatever movement is made for the collection of the revenue must be made by public order'.

Ireland comes in for the kill to directly implicate the Governor, asserting 'I want to show that this was a resistance to the irritation of a more frequent search, which was directed to be made by His Excellency when he was at the diggings'.

'Then I submit, your Honour, that this is not evidence' demanded the Attorney-General.

Defending his position as a matter of law, Ireland unequivocally stated, 'I certainly can go in to the state of the Goldfields and discuss the political question. In every political trial for high treason, the whole state of the locality is gone into.'

Justice Barry in a stern and forthright voice argued, 'Clearly so; but I conceive the personal direction of the Governor's cannot be admissible'.

Trying to settle the mood and stop this line of questioning the Attorney-General took a different approach. Instead he tried the tactful approach, responding quite politely and flatteringly to Richard Ireland, 'I beg my learned friend's pardon; I have no wish to fetter him in any way.'

The concerned Justice Barry stepped in to settle the matter. Thinking he was astute, Justice Barry noted, 'The subject is the collection of public revenue under a public Act of Council which is framed by the constituted authorities of this country and which must be considered as a public thing and I do not see myself what relevancy a personal visit of the gentleman who is Governor of this country can have with that.'

Ireland cleverly led his opponents into his shrewd plan, stating very plainly, 'Because he (being Hotham) gave a public order.'

An offended Judge, trying to keep control, demanded 'Where is this public order? – Do you think a policeman can give it? The witness has said the Governor visited the Gold Fields before; but anything emanating from the Government, with reference to the collection of the revenue, must be proved in the ordinary way.'

Ireland turns to Goodenough on the stand, rephrasing his question, 'Before this visit of the Governor's, was the collection weekly or monthly?'

'I do not know. I know it was collected weekly when I was there' Goodenough confessed under oath.

'And that was after His Excellency's visit?' Ireland asked.

'Yes' responds Goodenough, confirming under oath that after Hotham's visit, hunts were conducted once a week.

Not realizing where the brilliant Ireland was going with his line of questioning, Ireland takes it in another direction, 'On Thursday were you there when Mr Commissioner Rede went up amongst the people?'

'No' Goodenough recounted.

'Are you not aware that the troopers fired on the diggers on that day amongst the tents?' Ireland questioned. His strategy began to unfold. He sought to directly implicate Rede in shooting innocent people in a tent.

'I do not know; I was not present' Goodenough pointed out.

In a few short moves across the chess board on the courtroom floor, Ireland turned the tables completely on the government, implicating Hotham in the dastardly act of collecting taxes by military force, and Rede in the killing of innocent diggers. This clearly demonstrated to the jury that the diggers of Ballarat were merely protecting themselves from a tyrannous government.

The jury retired. Once again within thirty minutes the jury delivered the expected verdict of 'not guilty'. The frail looking Timothy Hayes was carried out of the courtroom and paraded through the streets by the over excited crowd.

The Queen v Raffaello Carboni

Hotham had done his dash. The cases against the rest of the diggers should have been dropped at this point. Unfortunately the Attorney-General believed they had a solid case against Carboni, therefore kept pursing what they called justice in the name of Queen Victoria.

Yet the government foolishly relied upon testimony of Andrew Peters and Henry Goodenough, who had already been discredited in the previous trials. Yet they pushed on.

The hanging judge, Justice Barry presided, along with the Attorney-General Stawell as the Prosecutor.

The defence was the young junior barrister named Butler Cole Aspinall with Richard Ireland, along with Joseph Dunne as Senior Counsel, who also represented John Manning.

The final jury selection consisted of tradespeople, farmers, gardeners and a grocer:

1. Phillip Bragg, of Cope Street, a farmer;
2. Alexander Bartholomew, of Brighton Road, a joiner;
3. James Black, of Greville Street, a butcher;
4. Charles Butt, of Lennox Street, a carpenter;
5. Thomas Bell, of Lennox Street, a carpenter;
6. Frederick Bainos, of Richmond Road, a painter;
7. Charles Belford, of Kewe, a gardener;

8. William Broadhurst, of Wellington St, a grocer;
9. John Bates, of Rowens Street, a baker;
10. Joseph Berry, of Hawthorn, a farmer;
11. David Boyle, of Kew, a gardener;
12. William Barnett, of Heidelberg, a gardener.[30]

The government trotted out the same old witnesses which did not influence the suspicious jury one bit. The witnesses asserted they had seen Carboni in the stockade with a pike, however this was John Robertson who was a mate of Carboni's. He did fight gallantly in the battle but died defending his mates.

Carboni insisted he was not in the stockade at the time of the attack. He further declared that he had never seen any of the supposed witnesses before, accusing the government of putting up false witnesses against him.

What did not go well for Carboni was the lack of witnesses to support his testimony though. Dr Carr was to appear but Carboni knew that John had sent him on a ship back to England. His resentment towards John ran deep.

With graphic detail, the shrewd Richard Ireland summed up for the defence by painting a picture for the jury of what would occur if they found Carboni guilty:

> If you the jury find this man guilty (pointing to Carboni), your decision will mean that under the law, Carboni's dismembered body will have to be hung from the gates of Ballarat.

The jury retired to deliberate the evidence before them. In an astounding turn of events the jury returned in about fifteen minutes. They found Carboni, 'not guilty'.

The packed courtroom could hardly contain their jubilation. Carboni in his true form went outside to make a speech, thanking his loyal supporters.

John Dalton came up to Carboni to shake his hand and Carboni side stepped him as if he was not even there.

John didn't utter a word but just gazed over towards him as he walked by. They never spoke again and every time John saw him on the streets of Ballarat in the following nine months, Carboni would cross the street rather than meet John face to face.

The government's attempt to hang the diggers of Eureka failed. Two of the ringleaders were acquitted and those still to go to trial were always going to go free, no matter what the government gave in evidence.

Each ruling within minutes of the jury retiring, came back with a verdict of, 'not guilty'.

It was so embarrassing, so devastating for Hotham and Stawell, that they decided to drop the charges against Australian born Thomas Dignum.

The entire proceedings were filled with corruption, perjury and malice on behalf of the government. All they achieved was making of mockery of the judicial system, which produced widespread resentment, proving their own incompetence in office.

Dalton's Gold
By Peter D Matthews

12
REFORMATION OF A NATION

In the words of John Thomas Dalton, 'Peter Lalor was the greatest man that ever lived'.

Peter Lalor and John Dalton had a special bond of friendship that was sealed with Lalor's own blood. Had it not been for the courageous quick thinking of John Thomas Dalton, Lalor if left behind as a wounded digger, would no doubt have become a pincushion for the bayonets of overzealous troopers.

Lalor would have been another name on the list of diggers killed that disgraceful Sunday, 3rd December 1854.

John risked his own life and limb for a reason. Not just because they were diggers together on the goldfields, but because there was something special about Lalor. It was almost as if John knew that Lalor had a destiny yet to fulfil - to change our great nation of Australia into what it is today.

Dalton's Gold
By Peter D Matthews

Tuesday 27th March 1855 was the last trial date set down in the Supreme Court of Melbourne. Instead the last digger, Thomas Dignum, was discharged without trial.

This same day coincided with the report of the Royal Commission Inquiry into the 'Conditions of the Goldfields of Victoria' being tabled in the Legislative Council.

By coincidence the report was 178 points long - exactly the same number of prospective jurors put forward by Hotham and Stawell. The scathing report was published in the Argus Newspaper in full on 30th March through to the 3rd April 1855, for all the citizens of Australia to read for themselves. The Commission concluded that the license fee along with the lack of political representation on the gold fields, and land issues, were the major grievances of the diggers.

Hotham opposed the findings of the Commission, however his closest allies did not share his feelings. Nor did Lord John Russell of the Colonial Office in London, who fully expected a local jury would not convict local men of high treason.

The Colonial Office were so concerned of completely losing control of the Victorian colony, that they rushed the granting of the Constitution of Victoria.

Every recommendation of the Royal Commission was implemented without delay. In April 1855 the gold diggers license fee was abolished and replaced by an export duty on gold at two shillings and six pence per

Dalton's Gold
By Peter D Matthews

ounce, with a yearly 'Miner's Right' to mine a claim with a fee of only one pound per year.

A raft of reforms swept through the state. Many of which were exactly what the diggers demanded back in November 1854, before the Eureka massacre.

The Legislative Council was expanded to include eight new mining representatives on the Council. The Goldfield Commissioners and half of the blue-pissants were sacked. They were replaced by one Warden of Mines and mining courts instead of a commissioner to manage disputes. Changes to the Goldfields Act of 1855 ratified the new changes which were effective immediately.

In the space of a few months the goldfields and the colony of Victoria was completely transformed - all because the diggers of Ballarat decided to stand together united against the tyrannous ruler of the day.

The Ballarat Reform League had petitioned the government to unlock the lands and make land available for miners to purchase. Why Hotham resisted until the shedding of blood, we may never know. The Royal Commission report recommended that land be released for private sale to diggers. Finally the diggers could put their roots down in a place they could really call home.

With what John had left of his gold from Dalton's Flat, after buying his own property at Smythesdale, he put in with a number of diggers from Ballarat to buy Lalor his own peace of paradise.

On 5th May 1855, Lalor attended a government auction at Ballarat and purchased the 160 acre farm in two lots for two hundred and sixty pounds. The land at Coghills Creek was only 16km north west of Ballarat heading towards Clunes.[31]

Even though the reward for Peter Lalor had been rescinded, he was still a wanted man. The Auctioneer asked the name of the successful bidder to record the purchasers details, when a loud voice shouted, 'Peter Lalor'. Many were expecting Lalor to give a false name. He came forward but to everyone's surprise, he was not arrested.

Within days the Attorney-General declared an amnesty on 9th May 1885, which meant that Peter Lalor and others previously wanted, could come out of hiding and walk the streets of Ballarat as free men.

John Dalton was a quiet and reserved fellow who hated the limelight, unlike Carboni. John preferred to be known as a boot maker, come farmer from Smythesdale that was too late arriving at the battle, rather than be known as an Irish rebel to which the government portrayed.

Lalor agreed to keep John's secret safe which was confirmed in Lalor's statement to the Argus clarifying what actually occurred. He withheld the name of John Dalton, noting the fellow who save him was a 'friend' and 'volunteer of the league'. Lalor had already told Phoebe Emerson and Stephen Cummings but John's secret was safe with them.

John didn't want the accolades for saving Lalor's life. He was merely doing his duty as part of the League and for his lifelong mate, Peter Lalor.

'He would have done the same for me' John would say.

John believed Lalor was the one who really saved the day. Had it not been for Lalor's command, John firmly believed that they all would have been slaughtered.

Rightly, the Commander in Chief, Peter Lalor should receive the accolades who united his mates for their own survival. John was merely the silent hero who helped in some small part, which ultimately resulted in reforming the nation. He was only one of many who helped make the country what it is today.

This was not the end of Peter Lalor but only the beginning. What would a disabled digger with one arm do with his life? He was educated as an engineer, son of a politician, an astute businessman, but without a shilling to his name.

The diggers of Ballarat handed the hat around and through fund raising they put together a substantial amount of one thousand pounds to set Lalor back on his feet. This in itself is evidence of the type of person Peter Lalor was. This amount of money was wages for the average person for ten years. This tells us the type of person he was. He was loved, respected and admired by all.

Lalor married Alicia Dunne on 10th July 1855 at St Mary's Catholic Church in Geelong, and moved back to the region of Ballarat to his Coghills Creek property.

With his mate John Phelan, they built a bluestone cottage and worked the farm together[32].

Dalton's Gold
By Peter D Matthews

Peter was an astute businessman. He had a share in many pies, and not just farming.

He had a share in many diggings at Ballarat, Smythesdale, Scarsdale and Clunes. Whilst he could not mine himself, he formed companies with many diggers across the region, including John Dalton at Smythesdale. Many of Lalor's companies employed Chinese diggers for cheap labour which later became well known in Clunes. Clunes is about 30km north of Ballarat and close to Lalor's home.

Meanwhile the Colonial Office ratified the Constitution of Victoria as an Act of Parliament on 16 July 1855 in the UK. This was a recommendation of the Royal Commission so that the English would retain control of the colonies.

The diggers of the little town of Ballarat now had the attention of the Monarch herself, Queen Victoria. Changes were implemented not just through Victoria but swept throughout all levels of government, right across the nation. The New South Wales Constitution Act 1855 was enacted on the same date and a raft of changes followed. This was the beginning of Australia moving towards becoming a democratic country.

The diggers of Ballarat never expected or planned such profound effects, like reforming the nation. They merely decided to take a stand to protect themselves and their way of life.

On 16 August 1855 the news of the Constitutional Act 1855 reached Victoria and in

November 1855 the diggers went to the polls for the first time.

Lalor was nominated to stand for the seat of North Grenville, in Ballarat. He was elected unopposed to the Legislative Council which launched him into a long and action-packed political career.

John Basson Humffray who was the president of the Ballarat Reform League was nominated to stand for the seat of Ballarat alongside Lalor and was also elected unopposed.

James Grant who was the solicitor who represented and signalled John Manning regarding jury selection at the state trials, was elected to the seat of Sandhurst on the Legislative Council.

On 28 November 1855 the changes took effect which started Australia on a long road of responsible self government. Are we there yet? In 2012, have we achieved responsible self government? Absolutely not, but we have come a long way since 1855. Or have we? That is another book altogether.

In less than a year after the Eureka bloodbath, the very diggers who had opposed Governor Hotham were now part of the Legislative Council.

As a military commander this result was more than a defeat. to Hotham - it was like Napoleon of France walking in and taking over England by request of Queen Victoria. In the eyes of Hotham these were foreign, predominantly Irish rebels, who had usurped the throne of England, but he as the Governor was powerless to act.

His mind could not come to terms with what had happened. He tendered his resignation in late November 1855. It is said that Sir Charles Hotham's, 'health was failing and on 17 December [1855]; he caught a chill while opening the Melbourne gasworks,'[133] and died fourteen days later on 31st December 1855.

At forty nine years of age, he was an accomplished naval commander having sailed all manner of seas and weather. In the middle of the most scorching time of the year in Melbourne, he was believed to have caught a chill that caused his death - I think not.

It is clear that Hotham died of a shattered heart. The very men that he went to war against, were now elected as part of his own government. Hotham could not bear such a thought.

The final day of 1855 recorded the death of Sir Charles Hotham. This day was remembered in history as the new beginning for the colony of Victoria, and as a result the entire country of Australia.

With the death of Hotham, the community closed the book and moved on. However many of the perpetrators who killed innocent men and women at Eureka were never brought to justice and those that were tried, were never convicted.

Captain Thomas who was the commanding officer at Eureka received the Maharajpoor Star, a self-indulgent medal of honour. It remains on display at Sovereign Hill Gold Museum. The brass six pointed star with red, white and yellow graded ribbon is presented in a rich red leather folder. It remains in original condition with the inscription:

> Captain Thomas was in command and participated in the action at Eureka Stockade on 3rd December 1854.

Not only was he given a medal of honour, but he was later promoted to the rank of Major-General. In 1881 he retired with the honorary rank of Lieutenant-General.[34]

Gold Commissioner Rede was kept on full pay from December 1854 until November 1855, when Hotham appointed him Deputy-Sheriff of Geelong and Commandant of the Volunteer Rifle Corps. This particular piece of legislation was assented as an Act of Parliament on 30th November 1854, just before the massacre. It almost seems now as if it was strategy planned that way from the beginning.

Rede later became Colonel of the Corps and rose to second in command in the colony of Victoria. It is rather appalling, having committed such premeditated mass murder, that he would be entrusted with such a position.

John Dalton only realized the connection Dr Carr warned him about in 1873, when Rede married Geraldine Clendinning who was the daughter of Dr George Clendinning. Dr Clendinning was the former partner of Dr Carr at the hospital. It took John Dalton almost twenty years after Eureka to realize that Dr

Clendinning was the spy in the hospital who was in bed with Rede.

Henry Goodenough, one would expect, would have been removed as a police officer for providing erroneous false testimony in the Supreme Court. Not under this government!

He returned to Melbourne as an officer, before being posted to the Geelong Police Station. He served alongside none other than Sheriff Robert Rede.

From there he was promoted to Senior Sergeant of the Bairnsdale Police Station where he died in 1890.

Clerk of the Court, Arthur Akehurst, who killed Henry Powell was acquitted of manslaughter by a Melbourne jury in the trial of Queen v Arthur Akehurst. It was presided over by none other than Chief Justice William a'Beckett on 18 January 1855. Justice a'Beckett ruled the dying man's testimony was, 'inexplicable as evidence', therefore could not be relied upon.

Akehurst was also transferred to none other than Geelong, where he served as the Clerk of the Court with his cohorts Rede and Goodenough. He was later promoted from one position to another. He worked as the President of the Board of Public Health and in the culmination of positions, became Secretary of the Crown Law Department of Victoria in 1890. He died at St Kilda in 1902 of bronchitis.[35]

Peter Lalor was very a different man. He lived the rest of his life for the people of Victoria, just as he promised when he swore an oath under the Southern Cross.

Dalton's Gold
By Peter D Matthews

Peter Lalor stood before the Legislative Assembly in Melbourne stating, 'if democracy means opposition to a tyrannical press, a tyrannical people or a tyrannical government, then I have ever been, I am still, and will ever remain, a democrat'.[36]

The Argus described Lalor as, 'a bluff, straight forward gentleman who blurts out plain truths in a homely matter-of-fact style'.[37]

Lalor continued in both private business and as a member of Parliament. He operated as a land and mining agent along with sitting on the board of several mining companies as a director. One of the most notable was companies was the New North Clunes Goldmining Co to which he partnered with John Thomas Dalton and James Edmund. James was a digger who also fought alongside John and Peter at Eureka.

They established the Clunes Water Commission with Peter Lalor as Chairman. This Commission supplied the water for the turbines to New North Clunes Goldmining Co and also supplied the water supply for the Clunes community. The government later purchased the water commission for £65,000 making it a rather profitable business. The Ballarat Star described the profitability of the company that year as, 'the largest dividend ever paid by a mining company'.[38]

Lalor was elected member of Parliament for South Grant in 1874 and continued to fight for the people of his electorate throughout his entire career. He became Postmaster General and Commissioner for Customs in Victoria. He attempted to remove the border between Victoria and New South Wales where he came head-to-head with Sir Henry Parkes. Parkes became the Premier of New South Wales and was notable for his famous speech in Tenterfield on Friday 25th October 1889, regarding the Federation of Australia.

Lalor became Speaker of the House in the Victorian Parliament in 1880 and held that position until his retirement in 1887. Although opposed by Thomas Bent who spoke of Lalor as a 'rebel against the British crown', he was regarded by many as the most impartial speaker that the Victorian Parliament has ever had.

Lalor declared in Parliament, 'The first duty of a Speaker is to be a tyrant. Remove him if you like, but while he is in the chair obey him. The Speaker is the embodiment of the corporate honour of the House. He is above party. He is the greatest representative of the people.'

That is the embodiment of the life of Peter Lalor - the greatest representative of the people, hence John Dalton naming him, 'The greatest man that ever lived'.

Twice he was offered knighthood by the Crown and twice he refused the honour. Lalor's only regret was being defeated on the floor of Parliament early in his career by John Fawkner. Fawkner was a friend and supporter of Hotham, who requested the Legislative Council budget one thousand pounds to erect a monument in honour of Hotham.

Peter Lalor opposed the motion, stating, 'Hotham had a sufficient monument in the graves of those slain at Ballarat'. The motion was passed on 10th January 1856 despite Lalor's opposition and the thousand pound budget was set.

The monument insignia reads, 'To the memory of Sir Charles Hotham Captain in the Royal Navy and one of Her Majesty's naval aides de camp Knight Commander of the Most Honourable Military Order of The Bath and the first Captain-General and Governor-in-Chief of Victoria'.

Lalor vowed to never visit the grave and to the author's knowledge, he never did.

This brings me to the latest monument recently erected by the government of Victoria - the Eureka Centre at Ballarat. The monument is about to be renamed the 'Australian Centre for Democracy at Eureka', after a ten million dollar redevelopment plan to 'promote a better understanding of Australia's history, particularly its democratic traditions'.[39]

What would Peter Lalor say to such a monument being erected when it heralds the Eureka Spirit as 'a synonym for democracy, the 'fair go' Australian-style, with the Eureka flag as the symbol of that spirit?'[40]

With many of the details polluted, tainted, incorrect and seeping of political propaganda, the memorial would no doubt offend such diggers as Peter Lalor and John Thomas Dalton.

The Federal Government have committed ten million dollars of taxpayer's money, asserting this Centre 'will promote a better understanding of

Dalton's Gold
By Peter D Matthews

Australia's history, particularly its <u>democratic traditions</u>.'[41] (underline mine)

The Eureka Spirit should never be eroded as a cry for a 'fair go', pushing the Labor Party's wheelbarrow. Nor should the events of Eureka be belittled to merely 'democratic traditions'. It was this sort of obnoxious government piety that led to the massacre of Australian diggers in the first place.

Clearly the defining moment in history should be remembered in the true light of day, without polishing, without massaging, without politicizing, without bias, just as Peter Lalor would.

The government of Australia went to war against every day Australians - people of all walks of life and professions, such as: doctors, lawyers, miners, shopkeepers, and tradespeople. The diggers cried out for tax reform and protested at the government's brutal method of collection. Instead of correcting their mismanagement of money, the government launched a premeditated overwhelming strike against Australian diggers, turning the gold filled valley into a valley flowing with Australian blood - all in the name of taxation.

This is really what occurred. It should be presented in its full truth, blood and all!

Many of us are sickened when we hear of 'conflict diamonds' or 'blood diamonds', where African diamonds are mined to fund oppression and atrocities on their own people.

Yet this happened to our forefathers in our own country, by our own government. Today the government are building a monument based upon a political spin in the effort to teach our children false information about the government orchestrated bloodbath. Get this though, this slanted political perspective is being incorporated into the school syllabus and children are flocking from all over Australia to visit the monument AND pay a fee to see and hear a politicized interactive display.

So even Peter Lalor's great, great, great grandchildren will now have to pay an entry fee to the government to see how their ancestors were persecuted and slaughtered by those in authority.

I wonder what Peter Lalor would say about this monument since he objected to a monument in honour of Sir Charles Hotham?

This defining moment in history on 3rd December 1854, should be remembered as a day of genocide against the Australian people, who courageously stood side-by-side unto death, having sworn an oath under the Southern Cross to defend each other from whatever tyranny or peril they faced.

In February 1889, Peter Lalor reflected over his life. In thinking of what happened at Eureka, he said:

> Tis better as it is now. We not only got all we fought for, but a little more. It is sweet and pleasant to die for one's country, but it is sweeter to live and see the principles for which you have risked your life

triumphant. I can look back calmly on those days. We were driven to do what we did by petty malice and spite.[42]

13
FOREIGN REBELS OR PIONEERS

Historically the government termed the diggers of Ballarat, 'vagabonds' and 'foreign rebels'. Many historians today present this same unbalanced perspective, seemingly to try to mitigate the government's actions in the massacre. They present the diggers as a motley crew of foreigners, mainly Irish, who went to war against the government from their fortified fortress, which we know was never built as a stockade.

Upon reflection where were most of the government officials, military and troopers from? Governor Hotham was an English naval commander who only emigrated to this native land of Australia a few months before the attack. He was a servant of the Queen but yet still a new immigrant, just as many of the diggers were some years before.

In fact John Thomas Dalton, like many of the diggers, came to Australia in search of new land, a new life, and perhaps even love. Many of his mates on the goldfields brought their entire families over to Australia to start a new life. There was but a few that came just to dig for gold and planned to return to their country of origin, taking with the their spoils.

John could only think of two people that came with foreign intentions. Raffaello Carboni never intended staying in Australia. Every time he found gold, he would send much of it back to his home land of Italy, declaring one day he would return.

When Carboni was released from the court, he returned to Ballarat. He returned for one purpose - to write his novel titled, 'The Eureka Stockade'. From John Dalton's perspective, this book was, 'Written merely to exonerate his own shortfalls'.

The book was self published in October 1855. Soon after completing it, Carboni departed Australia and never returned. He travelled Europe working as an interpreter for the French military and Italian politicians, passing away in Rome on 24th October 1875.

The second person was John Manning, who was much like Carboni. He was one of the thirteen charged with high treason.

After his acquittal, he emigrated to New Zealand and cofounding the New Zealand Celt magazine until he was arrested for sedition. Moving on to the United States he wrote about the Australian Goldfields and New Zealand. His writings were the same inflammatory style as those published earlier in the Ballarat Times, to which the owner Henry Seekamp was gaoled.

John Joseph was offensively termed a 'nigger rebel' from America. After his release, he was allowed to walk the streets of Melbourne as a free man. Joseph was no longer an American, having been shunned by the American Consulate. He was a real Aussie who fought with his mates. He went back to collect his belongings from Ballarat, then moved on to the Bendigo goldfields and continued as a gold digger until his death.

In 1858, Joseph was taken to the Bendigo Hospital after collapsing with chest pain on the diggings. Dr John Stuart tried to resuscitate John Joseph, however this proved unsuccessful. After an autopsy, it was found he died of valvular heart disease on 24th July 1958[43]. His death certificate confirms being born in America and arrived in Australia in 1852.

Many historians and genealogists attribute a grave in 1900 in Ballarat to this John Joseph, however the family of this Caucasian English gentleman, similarly named John Josephs, with an "s", confirm this person was born in Whitechapel and married Emma Jane Barnett in 1855.

There is no death certificate for a John Joseph any time around 1900 throughout the Colony of Victoria, which confirms John Dalton's account and the author's research.

Sydney born Thomas Dignum was discharged without trial. Rumour has it, he moved back to New South Wales and became a farmer.

Timothy Hayes after being acquitted did return to Ballarat, despite many historians asserting he travelled extensively and never returned. He worked as Ballarat East's Town Inspector for Nuisances. He later did travel extensively, making a name for himself as a military engineering expert. But he did return to Victoria and worked for the Railways. He eventually passed away in Melbourne on 31 August 1873.

Jan Vennik was originally of Koedijk, Netherlands. After his acquittal, he returned to the diggings of Ballarat. He spent the next eleven years as a miner at Ballarat. On 23rd March 1866, he married Kate Lucas (nee Kaatje Dekker), former wife of Andreas Lekatsas (English Andre Lucas), a shopkeeper at Ballarat.[44] It is not known why, but they moved to Melbourne at the same time as Andre Lucas, settling in Williamstown. Lucas and his family operated the first and finest Greek Restaurants in Melbourne.[45] Vennik and his wife then travelled via England back to Rotterdam, where Jane (or Kaatje in Dutch) was from, which is also not far from where Jan was born. They remarried on 17 March 1870[46] in the Netherlands to solemnize their marriage in their birth country, with their families as this was tradition. Although a death record cannot be found for Jan Vennik, most likely due to his name being repeatedly misspelled, it is believed he returned to Victoria and passed away in Melbourne.

James Beattie moved on to Benalla goldfields before marrying Mary Harrington. They had six children and became the pioneers of Nagambie, Victoria. He passed away from cardiac failure, accelerated by chronic Bright's (kidney) disease, on 30 November 1901.[47]

James Campbell, born in Renfrewshire, Scotland was a rather dark skinned Scotsman. Many of the diggers joked about his dark appearance with dark curly black hair, that he was really Jamaican, however he was born in Scotland in 1824 and arrived in Geelong on the Childe Harold on 16th July 1853.

After his acquittal, Campbell moved on the Castlemaine and Creswick goldfields, marrying Mary Millar and passed away at Daylesford, Victoria on 18th August 1881. They had one daughter, Mary Campbell, who in turn married John Cooper and together they had thirteen children, pioneering the Daylesford region of Victoria.

Henry Reid continued working all of his life on the goldfields of Ballarat, settling at Berringa with all of his children also working as miners into the 1900's.

Michael Tuohey as a young Irishman emigrated to Australia at the age of 19 in 1849. He was born in Scariff, Ireland in 1830. After his acquittal, he returned to the goldfields of Ballarat. He married Mary Green in 1873 and turned his hand to farming at Ballan, only 35km east of Ballarat. They had one son, Michael James Tuohey who was born in Ballan in 1878. Michael senior died on 10 September 1915 after breaking his thigh which was complicated by pneumonia.[48]

Jacob Sorenson, originally a Norwegian Jew, emigrated to Australia as a boy, therefore was Australian. After Eureka he moved to Casino, New South

Wales and worked as a farmer. He married Mary Kellaher who was born in Casino. They had eight children, one being the famous writer, Edward Sylvester Sorenson.[49] The Sorenson family became pivotal pioneers of the Northern Tablelands region around Casino and many generations still reside there today.

William Molloy and his brother Thomas arrived at Geelong on the ship Ben Nevis in January 1853 from Kings County, Ireland. After his acquittal, he returned to Ballarat. He spent the rest of his life working on the goldfields as a digger and labourer for other mining companies. He never married and passed away with an abscess on his liver, on 28 June 1884 in the Ballarat Hospital, aged 54.[50]

John Phelan, the business partner of Lalor, ran the farm at Coghills Creek. He married Mary Gillespie in 1861 at St Alipius Catholic Church in Ballarat. Phelan worked with Lalor until 1865 when he purchased land at Cobrico, Victoria, and started his own dairy.

John Phelan passed away in 1874 leaving Mary to raise her six children alone. In the most arduous circumstances, she worked the farm in true pioneering spirit. She was known to be driving a team of four bullocks with a baby in a shawl on her back, and walked eight miles across rough paddocks just to get to church.[51]

These diggers and their wives were true pioneers of Australia. They came here with hope of a new life and a great place to raise a family. The majority of diggers stayed in Australia, spreading right across this vast continent as pioneers, pivotal in their respective communities.

Many of them became Members of Parliament, members of local Councils, and quite notable people in Australian history. They were far from being 'foreign rebels' as asserted by the government.

John and Margaret Dalton became the pioneers of Smythesdale. They purchased a considerable amount of land along the main street and opened a boot makers shop on Brooke Street, Smythesdale.

John Dalton was involved in mining on a large scale with Peter Lalor at Smythesdale, Scarsdale, and Clunes. John had many sites around the region including Brown's Gully. He was instrumental in the armed conflict in 1859, after the government leased a portion of the Deep Lead to the Great Britain Company.

John was arrested early September 1859 and thrown in the Smythesdale lock-up. His mates raged with anger, demanding his release, threatening to demolish the lock-up to free him. The next morning, his lifetime friend John Lynch, negotiated with the police for his release without charge.

John Lynch was a digger who fought alongside John at the Eureka Stockade and moved to Smythesdale in January 1855, after John and Margaret Dalton. Their families intermarried and many of John's children and grandchildren were born in the Lynch's home. As there was no hospital in Smythesdale, the Lynch's home was used as a makeshift midwifery hospital.

John Dalton lived in Smythesdale for the rest of his life and passed away on 11 December 1897 at aged 65, from cancer.[52]

Leaving behind was his wife Margaret and eight children all of whom were born in Smythesdale. They had eleven children in total but three died in infancy.

Margaret Dalton Jnr was born in 1860 at their home in Smythesdale. She never married and died in 1939 in Scarsdale, only a few kilometres away from their original home.

Peter Dalton was born in the Brooke Street shoe shop in 1862, so rightly so, he became a shoemaker and was apprenticed to his father. He ran the shoe shop until his death in 1939. The old weatherboard shop was located on the right hand side of Brooke Street as you drive into Smythesdale from Ballarat, before the old gaol. It has since been demolished.

Peter also worked with his brother in the families mining businesses, while he sat as a local Councillor for many years. He was also Secretary of the Fire Brigade and President of the Smythesdale Homecoming Committee. He took a leading role in many local community organisations.[53]

Mary Ann Dalton was born in 1865 at Smythesdale. She married Thomas Dickson, a digger from Scarsdale. He worked for John Thomas Dalton 1st, and later became a director of the families mining businesses. They lived in Smythesdale all of their lives. Mary passed away 1937 at Ballarat, similarly her husband Thomas passed away in 1937 at Smythesdale.

Dalton's Gold
By Peter D Matthews

Their five children lived in Smythesdale and Ballarat and the Dickson family have since spread across the country.

Henry James Dalton, nicknamed Harry, was born in 1871 at Smythesdale. He married Alice Ellen Gilhooley in 1901. Alice was the daughter of Patrick Gilhooley, Mayor of Smythesdale and close friend of John Thomas Dalton. Patrick Gilhooley was one of the 114 arrested at Eureka but was later released without charge.

Sarah Jane Dalton born 1872 at Smythesdale, married William Mangles in 1898, a digger from Clunes. They lived at Leslie Street, Clunes and worked the Clunes diggings for the Dalton family businesses. They had seven children and the family were pioneers of Clunes.

Carolyn Ellen Dalton born 1873 in Smythesdale, nicknamed Nellie, never married and passed away at Scarsdale on 21st June 1943. She lived only 4km from the original home she was born in, on the very same street. She was a teacher at the Smythesdale school. Her body was buried in 1943 alongside her family in the Smythesdale Cemetery.

Alice May West was the youngest and longest living family of John Thomas Dalton. She was born in Smythesdale in 1876 and married Billy West in 1912. She lived to the ripe old age of 102 and died in 1978 in the Queen Elizabeth Centre, an Aged Care Facility at Ballarat. Her only son, William Dalton West. was originally a school teacher. He married Marjory Augusta Lade before going off to war. He was killed in the second world war, fighting in 58th/59th battalion of the Australian Army in Papua New Guinea.

William was trained at Seymour in Central Victoria. He arrived in Shrapnel Valley, near Port Moresby in March 1943. The division's ultimate destination though was the Lae-Salamaua front. William was flown to Wau then on to Bulwa and set on out foot along the difficult Missim Trail to take up position on Bobdubi Ridge, trying to capture Old Vickers. Old Vickers was the key to the ridge and its capture opened the way to Salamaua.[54]

On the 30th June 1943 the 58th/59th Infantry Battalion attacked the Japanese who poured the Aussie diggers with machine gun fire from fortified and camouflaged positions. Private William Dalton West was killed by Japanese fire in the battle to capture Old Vickers on 10th July 1943. His body was buried in the Salamaua War Cemetery - grave FA13. His name however lives on in the Australian War Memorial, Roll of Honour, Service number: V155879.[55]

This is the story of a real digger from a family of gold diggers, standing for Australia. He stood side-by-side with his mates, sacrificing his life, fighting for his family and friends way of life.

William West had heard of the valiant efforts of his grandfather, John Thomas Dalton, and headed off to defend his country to preserve our way of life. This is the true spirit of ANZAC shown right here in the history of the Dalton family.

Dalton's Gold
By Peter D Matthews

Alice left some memoirs of her family, including those of her son William, which were recently passed on to me. In 1976 her memoirs were also given to Assistant Researcher, Meg Barry, of the Sovereign Hill Museum, while Alice was still alive.

I was rather angered to find that despite being given the correct information, the Sovereign Hill Museum chose to ignore the facts of Eureka, hence my passion to right these errors.

John Thomas Dalton 2nd was born in 1868 in Smythesdale. With a name like his father, he became one of the most recognized gold diggers of Smythesdale. He married Emily Veronica George, daughter of Thomas George who was also a digger of Ballarat.

John Thomas Dalton kept a journal right throughout his life. Many of the treasures that I have gleaned as the author, have been confirmed in this ratty old black leather bound journal, given to him by his father but is now held together with duct tape to preserve it.

John Thomas Dalton 2nd was a farmer and chairman of mining companies that he established, including Canico Consols Co at Smythesdale.

He owned mining interests in North West Jubilee, New Jubilee, North New Jubilee, North New Jubilee Consols, Glenmona, West Berry Consols, Victoria United, Dry Diggings, Langi Logan South, North Langi Logan, Great Langi Logan, Central Extended, William Fancy, Cathcart Margaret, Cathcart Central, Lanberri's,

Dalton's Gold
By Peter D Matthews

Victoria United, North Golden Reef, Canico, South Frenchman's Specimen's Hill, North Canico, South Canico, Northern Territory, Clunes, Dalton's Flat, Canadian Gully, Linton, South Berry, Birthday Tunnel, Plateau Extended, Britannia Eclipse, Scarsdale, and even Creswick.

John Dalton was known, just as his father was, for producing the finest and cleanest gold in the region.

The Dalton's were also known to grow the best fruit and vegetables in Smythesdale. They owned quite a lot of land in Smythesdale, the amount unknown, but John Dalton recorded in his journal of owning 215 cows and 32 calves and a number of lots of land, so they were no doubt farmers as well as gold diggers.

John and Emily had five children. The youngest of them is still alive today at the ripe old age of 91. His name is William Leonard Dalton who was also born in Smythesdale.

He has fond memories of growing up in Smythesdale. He was best friends with Lloyd, the local policeman's son. Bill, as he likes to be called, married Gwen and worked as a meat inspector and moved away from Smythesdale. He moved to Portland, also in Victoria.

In 1970 he redeveloped his family farm at Portland, naming the street, 'Lalor Street'. Asking why he named it Lalor Street, he answered, 'I named it after the greatest man who ever lived - Peter Lalor'.

He affirmed the same statement his grandfather used to quote and my grandfather passed down to me.

Dalton's Gold
By Peter D Matthews

Actually, as I spoke with him on the telephone, William Dalton sounded just like my grandfather, Francis William Dalton. It was such a pleasure to talk with him. I could tell by the way he spoke to me that he holds the same ideals as those of his grandfather, John Thomas Dalton. His voice was soft, but yet firm. He exuded passion and fortitude, just like his grandfather.

Bill and Gwen have now lived in Cairns for almost forty years, but he still remembered every detail of Smythesdale. I was told by his son Peter, and his wife Denise, to speak slowly, clearly and especially loudly, because he was hard of hearing. I found his memory to be impeccable, recounting every detail just as my grandfather told me.

The ideals that John Thomas Dalton held on 3rd December 1854 are the same ideals held by the family today. Ideals such as honour, courage, humility and standing side-by-side despite the circumstances, is something that is entrenched.

The name of Peter Lalor will always be held in high esteem. Knowing that the Dalton family played some small part in reforming the nation, standing side-by-side with Lalor, is all that Bill need remember.

After all, had it not been for John Thomas Dalton, the nation of Australia would not be what it is today. Peter Lalor would not have survived, and the government would have remained without diggers representation. I can only shudder to think what our nation might be like if Lalor had not survived.

Today we still face a tyrannous government at times, but if we hold close the ideals of those who swore an oath under the Southern Cross, we just might change the nation for the better.

14
DALTON'S LAMENT

It was Saturday, 11th December 1897, and John Thomas Dalton laid in his bed at his Brooke Street home. He was exhausted and struggling to breathe. He had an aggressive cancer that had overtaken his now frail frame.

By his side was his wife of fifty-two years - little Margaret Carry (Carr). With her, was their sons Henry and Peter, along with daughters Margaret and Caroline.

While John laid upon his death bed, he reflected over his life.

'What would I change?' he thought.

He remembered leaving his mother and father in Canada and headed off to brave the high seas in search of gold; a new land; a new life; and perhaps even love.

Had he achieved all of his desires?

As he reflected, he certainly found a new land, and a new life on the goldfields. He found love the first time he laid eyes on his bride, Margaret, who stood by his side to that very day.

Dalton's Gold
By Peter D Matthews

Arriving on the goldfields, he was besotted with gold fever, which ran through the veins of all of his children. He found the Lady Hotham, yet his name was never recorded as the one who found it. The words 'unknown' written against the finder, sickened him to the very pit of his stomach.

There was only one real regret during his life and that was not speaking his mind at the time.

'Life is short' he reflected to his family, who were standing beside his bed.

John pondered for a moment. 'What would have happened if I had my gold licence on me at the time I went to see Rede. I knew better of Rede. Why didn't I take my licence?' John pondered.

'What would have happened if I spoke up at the time Scobie was allegedly murdered?' he deliberated.

'What if I spoke up about who really burned down the Eureka Hotel?' he thought.

'Maybe, just maybe, if I spoke up, the government would have stopped. But then again, they may have just shot me down on the spot.' John was perplexed.

'Always speak your mind. Never hold back' he uttered to his family.

As John Dalton saw his life flash before his eyes, he reminisced for a moment of his courageous efforts to save Peter Lalor. Instead of taking the secret to his grave, it was time to spill the beans.

He recounted what happened during Eureka so the world would know, that it was him who found the

Dalton's Gold
By Peter D Matthews

Lady Hotham nugget; it was him who saved Lalor; but it was also him who sent Dr Carr off in shackles to England.

He no doubt struggled to live with the guilt of not speaking up, but instead he laid the secrets of Eureka out before his family.

Struggling to breathe, he waved his right hand, calling Margaret in close.

In a small voice, he whispered into her ear, 'I have always loved you from the first time I laid my eyes on you.'

'I know, and I you' she replied, quietly sobbing.

He waved his hand, again calling the family in close and whispered to his children, 'I love you all, but it is my time. There is only one thing I ask of you - take care of your mother.'

With the last breathe his body could manage, preparing to meet his maker, his dying words were etched into a poem and penned by his family in their journal:

>In vain to live from age to age,
>While modern cards endeavour,
>I write my name in froze,
>And gain my poverty forever.
>If I get to paradise,
>And do not see your face,
>I'll pack my belongings,
>And seek the other place.

Dalton's Gold
By Peter D Matthews

    With the thought of standing for his mates at Eureka, having played some small role in changing the nation, he passed away peacefully on Saturday, 11th December 1897.

    Had he known his grandson, William Dalton West, I am sure he would be proud. Through my pen, the names of John Thomas Dalton and William Dalton West live on.

LEST WE FORGET

HISTORY CAPTURED

John Thomas Dalton
1832 - 1897

Dalton's Gold
By Peter D Matthews

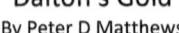

Margaret Dalton I (nee Carr)
1835 - 1917

Dalton's Gold
By Peter D Matthews

John Thomas Dalton II (son)
1868 - 1940

REFERENCES

[1] *Anderson, Tim,* **Bentley's Hotel Destroyed in 1854 - Ballarat in 1854 was a tent city**,
http://www.hereticpress.com/Dogstar/History/Bentley.html, accessed 22 January 2012

[2] The Argus Newspaper, Thursday 8 December 1854

[3] Carboni, Raffaello, (1855), **The Eureka Stockade,** reprinted www.freeread.com.au/ebooks/e00015.txt, accessed 12 January 2012, p25

[4] Ibid

[5] O'Brien, Paul, (1992), **Appendix 2: Uniforms of the Government Forces at Eureka**, Massacre at Eureka by Bob O'Brien, Australian Scholarly Publishing, ISBN 9781875606047, p156

[6] Ibid

[7] Ibid, p162

[8] Victorian Government, (1854), **Handbill - Social Order Notice**, Cultural Heritage Unit, The University of Melbourne, Eureka V.R. Notice. Government Camp, December 3rd, 1854 from Robert Rede, Resident Commissioner. Produced by the Times, Bakery Hill Ballarat. 1854, Collection Number: 89.0689 Courtesy of the Sovereign Hill Museum

[9] *Friends of St Kilda Cemetery Inc,* (Nov 2004) **Cemetery Conversations - Eureka**, http://www.foskc.org/pdf/CC16.pdf

[10] Fawcett, Jenny, **Arrests at Eureka**, Ballarat & District Genealogical Society Inc, http://www.ballaratgenealogy.org.au/art/witness.htm, accessed 7 March 2012

[11] O'Brien, Paul, (1992), **Appendix 2: Uniforms of the Government Forces at Eureka**, Massacre at Eureka by Bob O'Brien, Australian Scholarly Publishing, ISBN 9781875606047, p162-163

[12] Carr, Alfred, (1855), **Alfred Carr,** Coroners Report published in the Portland and Guardian Advertiser, 30 November 1855 after the death of Mary Carr.

[13] Ibid

[14] The Empire Newspaper, 23 November 1855

[15] The Argus Newspaper, Wednesday 18 February 1857

[16] Ibid

[17] Ibid

[18] The Ballarat Star, Thursday 29 May 1862, page 1 supplement

[19] The Age Newspaper, 14 February 1855

[20] Public Records Office of Victoria, (1855), **Eureka Stockade: Summary of the Trials of the thirteen Eureka prisoners charged with high treason**, VPRS 5527 Eureka Stockade - Historical Collection, http://www.access.prov.vic.gov.au/public/component/daPublicBaseContainer?component=daViewSeries&entityId=5527, accessed 15 March 2012.

[21] Public Records Office of Victoria, (1855) State Trials Transcript, Supreme Court of Victoria, The Queen v John Joseph, 22 March 1855

[22] Public Records Office of Victoria, (1855), **Eureka Stockade: Summary of the Trials of the thirteen Eureka prisoners charged with high treason**, VPRS 5527 Eureka Stockade - Historical Collection, http://www.access.prov.vic.gov.au/public/component/daPublicBaseContainer?component=daViewSeries&entityId=5527, accessed 15 March 2012.

[23] Public Records Office of Victoria, (1855) State Trials Transcript, Supreme Court of Victoria, The Queen v John Joseph, 22 March 1855

[24] Author Unknown (believed to be John Manning), The Ballarat Times, 18 November 1854

[25] Public Records Office of Victoria, (1855), **Eureka Stockade: Summary of the Trials of the thirteen Eureka prisoners charged with high treason**, VPRS 5527 Eureka Stockade - Historical Collection, http://www.access.prov.vic.gov.au/public/component/daPublicBaseContainer?component=daViewSeries&entityId=5527, accessed 15 March 2012.

[26] The Argus Newspaper, Tuesday 27 February 1855, p5

[27] Hotham, Sir Charles, (1855), **Eureka Stockade: Charles Hotham reporting the result of the trial of two of the Ballarat rioters, at the Supreme Court**, published by Public Records Office of Victoria, http://wiki.prov.vic.gov.au/index.php/Eureka_Stockade:Charles_Hotham_reporting_the_result_of_the_trial_of_two_of_the_Ballaarat_rioters,_at_the_Supreme_Court

[28] Bendigo Reform League, (1855), Eureka Stockade: **Bendigo Reform League call for the abandonment of the State Trial, published by Public Records Office of Victoria**, published by the Public Records Office of Victoria, VPRS 4066/P Unit 2, March 13,1854, http://wiki.prov.vic.gov.au/index.php/Eureka_Stockade:Charles_Hotham_reporting_the_result_of_the_trial_of_two_of_the_Ballaarat_rioters,_at_the_Supreme_Court

[29] Public Records Office of Victoria, (1855), **Eureka Stockade: Summary of the Trials of the thirteen Eureka prisoners charged with high treason**, VPRS 5527 Eureka Stockade - Historical Collection, http://www.access.prov.vic.gov.au/public/component/daPublicBaseContainer?component=daViewSeries&entityId=5527, accessed 15 March 2012.

[30] Ibid

[31] Corfield, Justin; Wickham, Dorothy; Gervasoni, Clare, (2004), **The Eureka Encyclopaedia**, Ballarat Heritage Services, Ballarat, Victoria, ISBN 1876478616, p319

[32] Corfield, Justin; Wickham, Dorothy; Gervasoni, Clare, (2004), **The Eureka Encyclopaedia**, Ballarat Heritage Services, Ballarat, Victoria, ISBN 1876478616, p319

[33] Knox, B. A., **'Hotham, Sir Charles (1806–1855)'**, **Australian Dictionary of Biography**, National Centre of Biography, Australian National University, http://adb.anu.edu.au/biography/hotham-sir-charles-3803/text6027, accessed 1 April 2012, first published in hardcopy in Australian Dictionary of Biography, Volume 4, (MUP), 1972.

[34] London Gazette, 18 November 1881, no 25039. p5620

[35] Dunstan, David, **'Akehurst, Arthur Purssell (1836–1902)'**, **Australian Dictionary of Biography**, National Centre of Biography, Australian National University, http://adb.anu.edu.au/biography/akehurst-arthur-purssell-12769/text23033, accessed 1 April 2012, first published in hardcopy in Australian Dictionary of Biography, Supplementary Volume, (MUP), 2005

[36] *Turner, Ian*, (2002), **'Lalor, Peter (1827–1889)'**, **Australian Dictionary of Biography**, National Centre of Biography, Australian National University, http://adb.anu.edu.au/biography/lalor-peter-3980/text6289, accessed 1 April 2012, first published in hardcopy in Australian Dictionary of Biography, Volume 5, (MUP), 1974

[37] Turner, Ian, (2002), ibid

[38] Turner, Ian, (2002), ibid

[39] The Eureka Centre, Media Release - Redevelopment 2009-12, http://www.eurekaballarat.com/redevelopment-2009-12.aspx

[40] The Eureka Centre Precinct, http://www.eurekaballarat.com/eureka/eureka-precinct.aspx

[41] The Eureka Centre, Media Release - Redevelopment 2009-12, http://www.eurekaballarat.com/redevelopment-2009-12.aspx

[42] Australian Icons - Ballarat, Outlook Productions Pty Ltd, http://www.australianicons.com.au/index.php?option=com_content&task=view&id=37&Itemid=68asp

[43] Death Certificate, John Joseph, Central District of Sandhurst (Bendigo), ref 1117, dated 24 July 1858

[44] Marriage Certificate, Jan Vennik, Central District of Ballarat, ref 613, 23 March 1866

[45] Andreas Lekatsas - Wikipedia.org, accessed 4 April 2012, http://en.wikipedia.org/wiki/Andreas_Lekatsas

[46] Marriage Entry Jan Vennik, Kaatje Dekker, Web: Netherlands, Genlias Marriage Index, 1795-1944 [database on-line]. Genlias

[47] Death Certificate, James Beattie, Central District of Nagambie (Shepparton), ref 376, dated 30 November 1901

[48] Corfield, Justin; Wickham, Dorothy; Gervasoni, Clare, (2004), **The Eureka Encyclopaedia**, Ballarat Heritage Services, Ballarat, Victoria, ISBN 1876478616, p512-514

[49] Kirkpatrick, Peter, **'Sorenson, Edward Sylvester (Ed) (1869–1939)', Australian Dictionary of Biography**, National Centre of Biography, Australian National University, http://adb.anu.edu.au/biography/sorenson-edward-sylvester-ed-8584/text14987, accessed 3 April 2012, first published in hardcopy in Australian Dictionary of Biography, Volume 12, (MUP), 1990

[50] Death Certificate, William Molloy, Central District of Ballarat, ref 18742, dated 30 June 1884

[51] Corfield, Justin; Wickham, Dorothy; Gervasoni, Clare, (2004), **The Eureka Encyclopaedia**, Ballarat Heritage Services, Ballarat, Victoria, ISBN 1876478616, p425

[52] Death Certificate, John Thomas Dalton, Central District of Smythesdale, ref 1390, dated 11 December 1897

[53] The Argus Newspaper, Thursday 4 February 1939

[54] Australian War Memorial, **58/59th Battalion (Essendon, Coburg, Brunswick/ Hume Regiment)**, http://www.awm.gov.au/units/unit_11335.asp

[55] Australian War Memorial, **Private William Dalton West**, http://www.awm.gov.au/collection/records/awm108/awm108-22-0435.pdf

Dalton's Gold
By Peter D Matthews

www.ingramcontent.com/pod-product-compliance
Lightning Source LLC
Chambersburg PA
CBHW031237290426
44109CB00012B/330